# TREVOR J. PARTRIDGE

# love with skin on

## THE GIFT OF YOUR JOURNEY

**paraclesis**
*Coming alongside others*

# Dedication

This book is dedicated to all those who have been a part of my journey. I am grateful for every person who has come alongside me and been the conscious presence of God in my life. Despite my own shortcomings, struggles and stumbles, they have taught and shown me much of Him, and He has been the constant supply of grace and truth through them. Their willingness to be there for me in the hard times is not only testimony of their faithfulness to the One they love and serve, but is also evidence of their readiness to be the reality of 'love with skin on'. I am forever blessed, and deeply indebted to them, and to my Lord and Saviour who saved me and made them part of my journey.

# Contents

# Foreword

I am a pastor of a five-year-old, growing church plant in Auckland, New Zealand, where we've been trying to do something new. We long to preach the authentic gospel, free from the cheap, tacky, cardboard-cut-out, easy-believism of so much modern Christianity. We long to restore 'community' to the centre of the gospel of Jesus Christ, the divine Son of the Father, who 'saved them for his name's sake' (Psa. 106:8, NIV). We long to be that people.

But longing and knowing how, are not the same thing. Wanting stuff and getting stuff are really two different things.

That's where my journey with a man called Trevor J. Partridge comes in. Trevor knows how to help people like me not only find community (which I found with Trevor) but also build community (something we did together). You see, if you want stuff, sometimes you have to have a wise guide – that's what Trevor is, a resource to the whole Western Church.

I want to commend Trevor Partridge to you as a man of integrity and honour, a man of virtue and conviction, a modern day Barnabas, a son of encouragement. Trevor doesn't just write, but he writes what he has really lived. That's why his prose drips with life-giving sweetness, like honey from the comb!

It is no mean boast to say that what Trevor has written in these pages is a modern day 'Acts of the Apostles' just to the extent that Trevor shows us how the power and grace of Jesus Christ, which manifests itself through people for people, continues even today in the Church in exile at the heart of the modern storm.

We might be at the ends of the earth here in New Zealand, 2,000 years after the gospel moved out from Jerusalem, but Trevor shows us in this excellent book how we still incarnate Jesus – with skin on – to the significant others around us, by treating the storms and stresses of our own story as a resource to share with others.

Better still, Trevor shows us this ecclesially – ie without ever leaving the important work of the Church of Jesus Christ behind. This is not abstract theology being platitudinously lay mouthed, but life-tested wisdom dug out of the heart of Church community together.

This book therefore is unique: not a counselling resource for the modern expert healers of the broken, so much as a playbook for Church life that acknowledges the sacred gift that is *every* saint's story. We really are – each of us – made strong at the broken places.

Trevor therefore shows us, as only he could do, how to break the bread of our lives and so feed the hungry around us, building up the body of Christ right where we are.

I could not recommend this book to you more as *the* definitive statement of Church life in the twenty-first century. I am honoured to write this foreword on behalf of a man and author who is not only a true and loyal friend but one of God's living saints for whom the truth is not a sales pitch or a punch-line but the pathway to the life of Jesus Christ in this present world.

If you are a church leader, buy a another copy of this book, for the one pastor-friend who will 'borrow' and never return it.

Rev Dr Craig Heilmann
Senior Pastor, The Upper Room Church
Auckland, New Zealand

# Introduction

At an early age my experience of church seemed normal for the post-war era. Sunday school was the order of the day, with weekly flannel-graph stories and a packet of Opal Fruits at the end for paying attention. Dad was a man of Christian character, a deacon, and a regular church attender who served the community through his position as a magistrates' clerk in the local town. It came as a complete shock to our family when Dad suffered what was then described as a 'nervous breakdown'.

I recall the day they sectioned him. My recollection is of two men marching him against his will down the hallway of our small home into the street to a waiting ambulance. Remembering a flannel-graph story from Sunday school, I shouted out after him in despair as they bundled him through the front door: 'Dad, always remember Job.'

They took him away to 'The Towers' psychiatric hospital. They were difficult days for our family, particularly my mother, as we adjusted to life with Dad not being there. 'The Towers' put him through the therapies of the day, including electro-convulsive therapy, drugs, and psycho-therapy, among others.

I vividly remember mum taking me to visit him; it's indelibly imprinted on my mind. The Towers was a foreboding place, built like a Victorian prison. I'll never forget seeing my distraught father there. This was my dad, who I regularly sat with in church on Sundays, singing gospel hymns, hearing the good news of God's love, that Jesus was the answer to all of life's problems. I learned a chorus, 'Christ is the answer to my every need, Christ is the answer He is my friend indeed, problems of life my spirit may assail, but with Christ as my Saviour I will never fail, for Christ is the answer to my every need.'[1]

In my young mind I now wondered, where was this answer so eagerly proclaimed on Sundays? I felt cheated and tricked. Why was the church unable to help and support my dad and my family whilst he, and we, were going through such a difficult, confusing time? I felt confused and perplexed by the pious platitudes and meaningless clichés that bore no relevance to the reality of my dad and family. It appeared that those in God's house didn't have a clue what to offer us. The warm and rosy-sounding Sunday gospel didn't appear to relate to our deep family predicament. It felt like there was no one to help us through. I wondered, is this the best the Church has got to offer?

During my teenage years I struggled to see the relevance of a gospel and Church seemingly powerless to meet the real needs and struggles of human lives. I knew God existed as an abstract notion but He just didn't seem to relate to the struggles of my world. In my mid to late-teens I wandered into Old Market Square in the centre of the city of Nottingham, where lunchtime gospel preaching took place, much like at Hyde Park Corner. It was where William Booth preached during his late teens as a Methodist lay-preacher before going to London to found the Salvation Army.

An older, white-haired man preaching that day caught my attention as hecklers barracked and sought to ridicule him. I was struck by the graciousness and compassion with which he appeared to respond to his mockers and detractors. At the end of his short talk, he gave an invitation, and something in him touched something in me. I found myself responding and raising my hand. John (which I later discovered to be his name) prayed with me and I said, 'Lord, I'm willing to serve You, but only if I can help people like my dad.'

On two or three days a week I'd meet up with John in that market square. At the close of his talk he'd spend 15–20 minutes sitting with me on the concrete plinth as I poured out my confused heart and troubled soul. He talked to me like a father, with compassion, wisdom, warmth, understanding and kindness. He would reassure me in my struggle and turmoil, take out his well-worn pocket Testament, sharing with me nuggets of truth and grace.

Over the days and months, John came alongside me as we journeyed together. As he poured grace and truth into my soul over those months, my broken heart was healed, my wounded spirit restored. He wasn't a church minister or pastor, just a regular local church member whose life had been touched by Jesus. A man of compassion, warmth, and godly wisdom, who knew how to journey with others as a fellow traveller.

My dad eventually came home from The Towers, and, after a long road to recovery, found faith enough to get back to as normal a life as possible. Years later, some months before Dad died, my wife Deb and I were with him in our kitchen. He rarely discussed that time in his life, but as we were generally talking he said, 'there is something I want to tell you. When I was in that dark tunnel of deepest despair in the hospital and I thought I'd lost my mind, I continually heard the words of a young lad calling out, "Dad, always remember Job." I held on to the words of Job: "I know that my Redeemer lives … Though he slay me, yet will I hope in him" and it sustained me in my darkest hour' (Job 19:25; 13:15, NIV).

Those days that I spent in the market square were the beginning of a journey that continues to this day. It set me on a quest that led me to try and understand how we can help struggling people like my dad in the Church. As part of my quest, I discovered the reality of *paraclesis* in New Testament Church life, and this is what I want to explore that with you in the following pages.

## CHAPTER 1

# Just show up and be there!

'Let us give thanks to the God and Father of our Lord Jesus Christ, the merciful Father, the God from whom all help [*paraklesis*] comes!' (2 Cor. 1:3, GNT)

A small boy was frightened one night during a large thunderstorm. The wind was howling and heavy rain was beating against his bedroom window, alarming and startling him. Terrified, he called out from his room, 'Daddy, Daddy, I'm scared!' His father, not wanting to get out of bed, called back, 'Don't worry, son, God loves you and will take care of you.' There was a moment of silence. Then the small boy sobbed back loudly, 'I know God loves me and cares, but right now, I need love with skin on.'

The journey of life can be like that at times: stormy, scary, turbulent, sometimes alarming and frightening. Life batters and bruises us all and we feel isolated and alone, needing someone 'with skin on' to be there for us.

## Hard times

I recall sitting in front of the consultant, thinking it would be a routine check-up following some regular tests. I noticed him intently looking particularly closely at the large screen in front of him. He cleared his throat and in a measured voice said, 'Something has shown up on your scan'.

Immediately I sensed deep down that something was wrong. 'Is it serious?' I asked. 'Very serious', he replied, 'you have a tumour the size of a grapefruit growing out of your left kidney'. 'Is it cancer?' I queried. '99.99% likely', he said, 'but it is too critical for us to simply do a biopsy.'

With that, he slowly turned the screen round to face me and I saw staring back at me, in stark reality, my kidney with a large misshaped growth attached. I winced in disbelief at what I was seeing. My immediate reaction was, 'This can't be right; I feel great, I'm healthy and fully active, I have no outward symptoms.' I protested, 'But I am due to fly back to Auckland in a week, where I am pastoring.' 'I'm sorry,' he said, 'that won't be happening. I'm sending you down immediately for your pre-med, ready for major surgery in a few days' time.'

So many questions began to race through my mind, and with this news, our world was thrown into a tailspin of confusion and uncertainty. Despite advances in medical care, the big 'C' word still carries dread, fear and trepidation. I sat there stunned, feeling as if I'd been kicked in the stomach. The next few days seemed a bit of a blur as we told family and friends, and came to terms with what this news would mean.

As I have already mentioned, we all go through hard times, some severe and unexpected. At times like these, like the little boy in the storm, we need 'love with skin on'. I knew the same God was with me after the diagnosis as before – He had not changed – but my circumstances drastically had. This wasn't a crisis of faith, but a crisis of life. My loved ones and I were now caught up in the maelstrom of a cancer storm with its own set of unfamiliar challenges.

## Coming alongside

My wife Deb and I were in uncharted territory in the difficult early days of adjustment to our new set of circumstances. We had full confidence in the medics, our faith – shaken but not shattered – was in our God. Even so, we'd been blindsided; we felt vulnerable, fragile and more conscious of our human frailty than ever. We needed fellow travellers to support, strengthen, encourage and share insight , not just the well-meaning gentle pat on the back with the reassuring words, 'don't worry, God's in control'. We needed those who'd walked this way before. So we talked to friends who had travelled this pathway before us. They became fellow travellers on the process of our journey. As they came alongside, journeying together with us and guiding us, we received courage, strength, faith, hope and grace.

The New Testament Greek word describing 'love with skin on' is *paraklesis*, from two Greek words – *para*: 'to be with', 'alongside'; and *kaleo*: 'to call', 'to come'. It literally means, 'to come alongside in time of need'. It's found in its various forms over 140 times throughout the New Testament. *The Message* translation best puts it in context: 'He comes alongside us when we go through hard times, and before you know it, He brings us alongside someone else who is going through hard times so that we can be there for that person just as God was there for us' (2 Cor. 1:4). The word *paraklesis* occurs five times here and another five in the next three verses. The strong, repetitious use is a clear indication of its significance. The anglicised transliteration is spelt *paraclesis*, taken from the Latin and French translation. My personal, consise definition of *paraclesis* is: 'Just show up and be there for someone who is struggling'.

*Paraclesis* is two-dimensional. Vertically, 'He comes alongside us'; then horizontally, 'He brings us alongside someone else', so that we can be there for that person just as God was there for us. As God reaches down to us, so we in turn can reach out and become His tangible presence in someone else's life, 'love with skin on'.

Help we receive from God isn't simply for our own benefit. Our hard times not only give us opportunities to receive His grace and comfort, but they open a door of opportunity to share our experiences with others. The verse in 2 Corinthians 1 directly connects our ability to help others with the help we receive. God's grace *to* us becomes God's grace *through* us. In this way, our struggles become a channel of grace to others in their adversity. Think back to those who've come alongside you, supporting, encouraging and helping you in hard times. Be thankful for them – they were part of God's plan for your life.

## Who Cares?

John McArthur of Grace Community Church says in his commentary on Philippians that *paraklesis* is precisely the kind of assistance exemplified by the Good Samaritan, who after doing everything he could for the robbed, beaten stranger, journeyed with him and took care of him at the inn, promising to repay the cost.[1]

In Luke 10:25–36 an impudent lawyer comes to Jesus enquiring, 'what must I do to inherit eternal life?' Jesus asks, 'What is written in the Law?' The lawyer responds, 'Love the Lord your God with all your heart … Love your neighbour as yourself.' Jesus replies, 'that's right, do this and you will live.' The lawyer, not finished, mischievously asks, 'and who is my neighbour?' (my paraphrase). Jesus' response results in the story about a man travelling on the Jericho Road. It's an allegory for the journey of life, a road we all travel, where people and life circumstances conspire to ambush, beat, bruise and wound us. The question that arises in such times is: who cares?

A priest and a Levite come by. Good, God-fearing, devout folk. People who regularly went to  church, who were either coming from or going to the Temple, because that's what they did. They were the religious of the day, occupied with temple duties. They come to where the assaulted man is but are so busy 'doing church', so focused on church activities, so wrapped up with the sense of their own high calling, that they pass him by on the other side. It's like saying a famous preacher, local pastor or vicar came across a wounded believer on the street but walked by and ignored them.

## An unlikely hero

Then, Jesus throws a grenade into this story. At the time, it would have been explosive. He said that a Samaritan came by, saw the man and went to his aid. To the Jew, 'neighbour' and 'Samaritan' were incompatible words. They just didn't fit together. It's an ironic statement Jesus makes, as Jews and Samaritans had no dealings with each other (John 4:9). Samaria was like the West Bank or the Gaza strip today, with the animosity and hatred existing between many modern Palestinians and Israelis. It was like saying, along came a terrorist from the PLO or Hamas, who stopped to help the man.

The Samaritan portrayed by Jesus is the unlikely hero. If anyone had an excuse to turn a blind eye and walk by, he did. He was despised, rejected as a religious outcast and stigmatised as a heretic. For the Jew of the day, there was no such thing as a 'good Samaritan'. It was a contradiction in terms; an oxymoron. The story underlines the failure of the priest and the Levite to 'come alongside' the stricken man and exposes their religious impotence and spiritual hypocrisy.

These devout church folk probably said, 'we're just so busy with church life, we'll just have to leave him'. If the priest and the Levite had reached out to this man where he was, there wouldn't have been a need for this Samaritan to do so. If religion means you don't have time for a dying man, what good is that religion? Unfortunately, generally speaking, Christianity and the Church is invariably the last place non-churched people think of turning to in time of need, because it appears to them it's too busy doing its own 'religious' thing, bearing little relevance to their world. I wonder sometimes, if to the non-churched, we really do look like 'love with skin on'?

The Samaritan saw what they saw, but his reaction was different. The priest and the Levite remained indifferent and detached, refusing to come alongside the stricken man. But something inside the Samaritan motivated him to stop, 'come alongside' and engage with this man in need. He felt something stronger than the fear of antagonism, hostility, rejection and the unacceptance of being a Samaritan. In spite of great risk, he stepped out of his comfort zone, crossed the street and got involved. It took great courage. He would have been the chief suspect. This was a no-go area for him but he chose to engage.

## A core value

By the way, Jesus never called this man a 'good Samaritan'. He is only described as a Samaritan. We call him good because his act of 'coming alongside' and journeying with the stricken man, his act of *paraclesis*, seems so exceptional that we think he was good, but the Bible doesn't say that. Just that he was an ordinary, regular Samaritan, who 'when he saw [the injured man], had compassion *on him* … and took care of him' (vv33–34). For this Samaritan, becoming 'love with skin on' was a core value. To the question, 'Who cares?', his response was, 'I do', and he willingly got involved in the bowl and towel ministry, tending the man's wounds. As *The Message* translation puts it, 'When he saw the man's condition, his heart went out to him'.

'Coming alongside' means ordinary people being willing to be a supportive presence on someone's troubled journey. 'That's exactly what Jesus did. He didn't make it easy for himself by avoiding people's troubles, but waded right in and helped out. "I took on the troubles of the troubled"' (Rom. 15:3–4, MSG). It's being there for someone in hard times, giving help, assistance, support, care and aid, just as God was there for us.

So here it is again, 'He comes alongside [*parakaleo*] us when we go through hard times, and before you know it, he brings us alongside [*parakaleo*] someone else who is going through hard times so that we can be there [*paraklesis*] for that person just as God was there [*parakaleo*] for us' (2 Cor. 1:4, MSG). *Parakaleo* is a word with legs on, a verb, active, saying something in order to achieve something. A 'present active participle', 'present', in the here and now; 'active', intentionally engaging; and 'participle', taking part through action. It urges us to get involved with those we've come alongside, making available to them whatever they need in their circumstances of life. 'Present tense' means ongoing, continually present, recognizing the need and giving active, practical help now, as the (Good) Samaritan did, 'taking care of him'. Caring as a core value means having the same care for others as we have for ourselves.

## Self-focused living

The antithesis, or opposite, of *paraclesis* is self-focused living. Paul exhorts the Philippians, 'Don't let selfishness and prideful agendas take over. Embrace true humility, and lift your heads to extend love to others. Get beyond yourselves and protecting your own interests; *be sincere*, and secure your neighbors' interests first. *In other words*, adopt the mind-set of Jesus the Anointed. *Live with His attitude in your hearts*' (Phil 2:3–5, TV).

Unfortunately, we live in a largely self-obsessed world of privatised individualism, every man for himself. It seems like we are currently consumed by the world of 'selfies' on social networks, and sharing the triviality of our lives from the privacy of our self-focused universe. Of course, social media can be used in a very positive, meaningful way to communicate, but it can also be abused.

I read the other day that in the UK, over 17 million selfies are uploaded to social media weekly.[2] This selfie addiction has now become a categorised condition catered for in addiction recovery clinics. It seems to me that our modern world has again become similar to the life of Narcissus from ancient Greek mythology, who knew nothing of this Greek word *paraclesis*. After seeing his own reflection in a pool, Narcissus became so absorbed with it that he fell in love with himself. Besotted and captivated, he was unable to leave his own reflection and died alone by the pool.

Thomas Carlyle, the Scottish philosopher and renowned historian, one of the most important social commentators of his time, said, 'Let me have *my* own *way* in exactly *everything* and a sunnier and *pleasanter* creature does not exist.'[3] We're all instinctively self-centred; it's our natural tendency as a consequence of our fallen-ness to be self-absorbed. From our earliest years, we learn to become the centre of our own universe. John Zizioulas, in his book *Communion and Otherness*, says 'Individualism is present in the very foundation of this culture. In our culture self-protection is a fundamental necessity. We feel more and more threatened by the presence of others. We are forced and encouraged to consider the other as our enemy before we can treat him or her as our friend. We accept them only in so far as they do not threaten our privacy, and are useful for our individual happiness.' [4]

## Others-focused living

Have you ever found yourself walking by on the other side without realising it, so caught up in the busyness of your own world that you just don't notice the struggle in someone else's? 'Coming alongside' means other-focused living. Paul puts it to the Galatians like this, 'everything we know about God's Word is summed up in a single sentence: Love others as you love yourself' (Gal. 5:14, MSG). Somehow the devout priest and Levite missed this bit of the Law.

Stephen Covey records a time when he was travelling on the New York subway. A man entered with some noisy, unruly children. He sat down and closed his eyes, oblivious to his rowdy offspring. The quiet subway car now became an atmosphere of rowdiness and chaos. The children's inappropriate behaviour became obvious to everyone except the father. Finally, Covey confronted the man about his children. The man opened his eyes, evaluated the situation as if unaware of it, and responded, 'Oh, you're right, I guess I should do something about it, but you see I've just come from the hospital where their mother died about an hour ago. I don't know what to do, I guess they just don't know how to handle it either.'[5]

The apostle Paul put it like this, 'None of you should be looking out for your own interests, but for the interests of others' (1 Cor. 10:24, GNT).

Similarly, someone once suggested we put a 'Neighbourhood Watch Area' sign in the foyers of our churches as a clear sign of our community awareness and support, showing that people in our church watch out for each other – they don't just mind their own business but look after the interests of others. For Jesus, love of God is expressed by love of neighbour, 'love with skin on'.

## Becoming love 'with skin on'

We regularly meet people burdened by life's issues. It's possible that, today or tomorrow, we may connect with someone who's life is falling apart at the seams but we may not realise it. Will Smith said, 'never underestimate the pain of a person, because in all honesty everyone is struggling. Some people are better at hiding it than others.' [6] Recognise that God has been preparing you in your own hard times to get alongside someone in theirs. The robbed man in the Good Samaritan story is a picture of people on the journey called life; left beaten up, bruised, battered and broken by life circumstances, needing someone to step beyond the self-absorbed living of the priest and the Levite. Who, like the Samaritan, will be there for them with compassion?

As with the Samaritan, 'coming alongside' is more an opportunity to be seized than one to be created. Opportunities don't make appointments; you have to be ready for them when they arrive. 'Love never gives up. Love cares more for others than for self' (1 Cor. 13:4, MSG). I recall sitting in my office one day when the cleaner came in to empty the waste paper basket. Making polite conversation, I asked, 'How are you today?' She replied with a heavy sigh in her voice and strained expression on her face, 'Not too bad.' 'Does that mean not too good?' I ventured, and with that she broke down in tears, telling me she'd come from her aunt's house, who had just committed suicide, leaving three teenage children. This became an opportunity for me to get alongside her and give support. Like the Samaritan, we are faced with opportunities to get alongside others every day.

The Samaritan Jesus spoke of, moved with compassion, reached out to this man with 'the gift of his journey' and its resources. The priest and the Levite remained indifferent and detached, staying on the safe side of the street, even walking by on the other side. Like the father in the middle of the night, remaining in his comfort zone, simply calling out what seemed to be a religious cliché and pious platitude to his son. In answer to the lawyer who asked the question, 'And who is my neighbour?' Jesus recounted this *Paraclesis* story, asking him 'which one was his neighbour?' He replied, 'The one who showed mercy' – 'the one who *came alongside*'. Jesus issued the challenge, 'Go and do likewise' (v37). I guess He also may have said to the father of the boy in the storm, 'Now you get out of bed and go and be my love "with a skin on". Go and get alongside the lad.'

Deb and I came through the storm; my current prognosis is good, classified as being in remission, and we're grateful to God for bringing 'love with skin on' alongside us in our hard time. People who had found God's grace more than sufficient in their hard time and were willing to pour that grace into us in ours.

## CHAPTER 2

# A missing jewel

'We then that are strong ought to bear the infirmities of the weak, and not to please ourselves. Let every one of us please his neighbour for his good to edification ... Now the God of patience and consolation [*parakalesis*] grant you to be likeminded one toward another according to Christ Jesus' (Rom. 15:1–2,5, KJV).

In the 2002 movie *My Big Fat Greek Wedding*, a romantic comedy about a traditional Greek family, the daughter Toula decides to marry a non-ethnic Greek. Father of the bride, Gus Portokalas, says to his future non-Greek son-in-law, 'Give me a word, any word, and I will show you the Greek root of that word.'[1] Consolation, encourage, comfort, exhort, entreat, advocate, help, plead. What do these words have in common? Well, in the words of Gus Portokalas, they're all different shades of meaning of the same root Greek word, *paraklesis*. As we've seen, the primary meaning of the word is *para*: 'to be with', 'alongside'; and *kaleo*: 'to call', 'to come', literally, 'to come alongside' (see 2 Cor. 1:3–4 for more about God's comfort).

But *paraclesis* has a much greater depth of meaning; it is much more far reaching. It's a difficult word to translate directly because unfortunately there isn't one word in the English language big enough to describe or convey its meaning. So the English New Testament uses these other words to capture its nuances, with the etymological meaning being shaped by its context and usage. It is *'coming alongside'* – not just to be there, but to be there for a purpose. These words help us to fully grasp the meaning and breadth of *paraclesis* in New Testament Church life. It's like looking at a diamond turning in a bright ray of light. As light shines on its various facets, different dazzling colours and hues are reflected from its surface. *Paraclesis* is such a word, and is a central tenet and theme in New Testament Church practice and life. I wonder, could it possibly be a missing jewel in the Church's crown?

## Your consolation has come

The second facet of the diamond (the first being 'coming alongside') is found nestling in the context of the Christmas story. A passage that is mostly overlooked, and rarely, if ever, found on Christmas cards or in nativity plays. It's lodged between the manger scene and the later visit of wise men. In Luke 2:25–30, at barely six weeks old, the Christ-child is taken by Mary and Joseph from Bethlehem to the Temple in Jerusalem for consecration in accordance with Old Testament scripture. At the Temple, 'there was a man in Jerusalem whose name was Simeon, and this man was just and devout, waiting for the consolation [*paraklesis*] of Israel, and the Holy Spirit was upon him' (v25).

As Simeon catches sight of the Christ-child swaddled in his parents' arms, his eyes widen, his gaze transfixed as his heart leaps within him. He is in the Temple waiting for the 'consolation of Israel'. Reaching out, he scoops up the baby, receiving 'the consolation of Israel' into his arms, giving thanks to God. This is the moment he has waited for, longed for, prayed for all his life. He is overwhelmed with wonder, joy, astonishment; the Word has become flesh, the *paraklesis* of Israel has come. He catches his breath and makes this proclamation, 'Lord, now you are letting your servant depart in peace, According to your word; For my eyes have seen your salvation' (vv29–30). He consecrates and blesses Jesus in God's House as Mary and Joseph marvel at this momentous declaration. As *The Message* puts it, 'The Word became flesh and blood, and moved into the neighborhood' (John 1:14).

How I'd love to see this scene back on our Christmas cards and in nativity plays. It's traditionally known as Simeon's Song, the Christmas Canticle, *Nunc Dimittis*, a rarely heard beautiful declaration of God's salvation to the world. It ranks alongside Mary's Song, The Magnificat: 'My soul doth magnify the Lord, And my spirit hath rejoiced in God my Saviour' (Luke 1:46–47, KJV). This missing Christmas scene is of huge significance. 'The consolation of Israel' is an Old Testament description of the awaited Messiah, Jesus the Christ. Israel had been waiting centuries for the 'consolation' [*paraklesis*] of God to arrive. Isaiah had proclaimed the coming Messiah, 'unto us a child is born … a Son is given … And his name will be called … Prince of Peace' (Isa. 9:6). The angel announced His arrival, 'they shall call his name Immanuel … "God with us"' (Matt. 1:23) and here in the temple Simeon introduces Jesus the Christ, the Divine *Paraklesis*, 'your salvation' (Luke 2:30).

First and foremost, *paraclesis* means the active presence of Jesus Christ sent from above, coming alongside, God with us, bringing the salvation of God. He is the Christ of consolation. Paul said, 'our consolation [*paraklesis*] also abounds through Christ' (2 Cor. 1:5). Consolation is the presence of peace, joy, grace, light, hope and salvation. The greatest consolation we can have is to know that salvation has come to us in the person of Jesus, the Christ. Salvation and consolation (*paraclesis*) go together.

Paul, writing to the Corinthians in the light of this says, 'Now if we are afflicted, *it is* for your consolation [*paraklesis*] and salvation, which is effective for enduring the same sufferings which we also suffer. Or if we are comforted [*parakaleo*], *it is* for your consolation [*paraklesis*] and salvation. And our hope for you *is* steadfast, because we know that as you are partakers of the sufferings, so also *you will partake* of the consolation [*paraklesis*]' (2 Cor. 1:6–7). The message of consolation to the troubled, the weak and struggling is, 'your consolation has come'.

Bringing consolation to others is bringing the presence of Jesus, the Prince of Peace, Christ in us; giving solace and hope, allaying fears, calming storms, easing stress, soothing hurt and bringing rest to the restless. This isn't consolation in the shallow, patronising sense in which we use the word: 'Well, if it's any consolation, I'm suffering too.' It's entirely the opposite! How often in Scripture does the Lord reassure one of His servants with consoling words, 'Do not be afraid, for I am with you'. C.H. Spurgeon said, 'Consolation is the dropping of a gentle dew from heaven on desert hearts beneath. True consolation, such as can reach the heart, must be one of the choicest gifts of divine mercy.' [2] Consolation leads to the next facet of the *paraclesis* diamond – encouragement (*parakaleo*).

## Jump leads at the ready

One morning I got up to head off to the church office, put the key in the ignition, and with a whimper and a burp, my car refused to start. The engine just wouldn't turn over no matter how much I kicked the tyres and banged the steering wheel. There was nothing wrong with the car except the battery refused to respond to my frustrated demands. With a busy day ahead, I felt that sinking feeling of realising your battery is dead. And that's how life is sometimes. All seems well, then suddenly out of the blue our batteries go dead. No matter how much we kick the tyres and bang the steering wheel, spiritually, emotionally, relationally, physically, vocationally, there just seems to be nothing there; we find ourselves flat, on empty.

Not being a member of a roadside service, I realised the only way to get out of this was to get another car with a running engine to come alongside my car and jump start me. I called a friend, and within the hour he was there with his jump leads, connecting my lifeless battery to his revving engine. Within seconds there was a surge of much needed power and energy; my engine burst into life, firing on all cylinders. My friend became my consolation, salvation and encouragement. He got me going on my way again. So the first step on the *paraclesis* journey is through the jump leads of consolation and encouragement. Our engine restarts with an infusion of strength and energy into the 'dead batteries' of our spirits. Paul, speaking of Timothy, says, 'His mission was to strengthen and encourage [*parakaleo*] you in your faith' (1 Thess. 3:2, GW). The injection of encouragement brings vitality and fortitude, it provides a power surge, a boost enabling us to get going again, to keep going when we stumble. Consolation and encouragement restore our sense of 'get up and go', after it has got up and gone. Like putting petrol in the engine.

'Encouragement' literally means to put in courage, to hearten, to inspire. It describes infusing someone with fresh confidence, hope and wellbeing, filling them with strength and optimism. 'Inspire' literally means to breathe in new life, to energise, to fill with grace. William Arthur Ward said, 'Flatter me, and I may not believe you. Criticize me, and I may not like you. Ignore me, and I may not forgive you. Encourage me, and I will not forget you.'[3]

## Coming alongside

The initial step of encouragement is a willingness to get alongside. 'Gently encourage [*parakaleo*] the stragglers, and reach out for the exhausted, pulling them to their feet. Be patient with each person, attentive to individual needs' (1 Thess. 5:14, MSG).

I'm an armchair sports fan. How I would love to have the skill and energy to participate in many of the sports I watch. Maybe, like me, you've watched the London marathon from the comfort of your armchair. Once the profesionally trained and experienced runners have come through, the fun runners and ordinary enthusiasts arrive. I'm always impressed by the tens of thousands that run and strive to complete the course – most running to raise money for charity. The stragglers struggle to the finishing line, flagging and exhausted, barely able to make it.

If you watch them as they come to the final straight on Westminster Bridge there are crowds eagerly awaiting, looking for their friends and loved ones as they drag themselves towards the finish line, drained, gasping and spent. You see family, friends and bystanders coming alongside the barrier, gently jogging beside them, shouting, cajoling, clapping and cheering them on. Willing them, motivating them, inspiring them, spurring them on to make it all the way.

What if they shouted 'give up', 'you'll never make it', 'you're too exhausted', 'quit before you collapse'? How would they feel? I've even heard myself on occasion shouting at the television screen, 'come on, mate; you can make it – keep going!' Surely the Church should be the place where we're cheering each other on and cheering each other up every Sunday. Paul writes, 'we … sent Timothy to get you up and about, cheering you on [*parakaleo*] so you wouldn't be discouraged by these hard times. He's a brother and companion in the faith' (1 Thess. 3:2, MSG).

## Oxygen for the soul

Something happens when we're encouraged; our flagging spirits are lifted, buoyed and bolstered by affirming words and supportive deeds. Often we've no idea how a simple gesture of encouragement can rekindle purpose and strength to the weary and careworn.George Adams said, 'We should seize every opportunity to give encouragement. Encouragement is oxygen for the soul.' [4] A study was done by psychologist Dr Henry H. Goddard on energy levels in children.[5] He used an instrument called an 'ergograph' and somehow he managed to get children standing still long enough to connect them to the machine. His findings are fascinating. He found that when tired children are given a word of praise, affirmation or encouragement, the ergograph showed an immediate upward surge of new energy. When the children were criticized and discouraged, the ergograph showed their physical energy took a sudden nosedive. It is probably true to say the same of adults. When we're encouraged, our energy levels go up; when we're discouraged they go down.

## A daily exercise

'Encourage each other every day' (Heb. 3:13, GW). Encouragement is something we all can give. People we meet every day are often struggling more than we realise, even those at the petrol station, the bus stop and supermarket till. Be aware and alert to the opportunities that present themselves every day. I once read of an audience at a concert who had just finished hearing a solo by a squeaky tenor. When he finished the applause was less than enthusiastic, but one member of the audience exclaimed, 'Extraordinary! Wonderful!' 'Excuse me', said a puzzled man in the next seat, 'I can claim some knowledge of the subject, and I think his voice was very poor.' 'Voice?' replied the other man, 'I wasn't thinking of his voice. I was praising his nerve!'

Encouragement doesn't always come naturally because we tend to see the negative and miss the positive. The American Standard Version of the Bible says, 'not looking each of you to his own things, but each of you also to the things of others' (Phil. 2:4). Encouragement is like a muscle needing regular daily exercise. The more we exercise it, the stronger it becomes, and we find ourselves doing it without thought or effort, not now and again or occasionally, but regularly.

## Take the initiative

'Therefore encourage [*parakaleo*] one another' (1 Thess. 5:11, NIV). We shouldn't wait for others to encourage us but take the initiative to be a jump lead ourselves, even when others aren't encouraging us. Many times, a thoughtful word, act of thanks, appreciation or kindness has helped a struggling soul to stay on their feet and keep going. I have heard a story about a boy who loved music and was bitterly disappointed because he could neither play nor sing. One day he shared his disappointment with Amati, a violinmaker, who said: 'There are many ways of making music. Some play violins, some sing, some paint pictures, some carve statues, while others till the soil and grow flowers.

Each person sings a song and helps to make the music of the world. You can make music too.' And so, Antonio Stradivari grew up to make music by also making violins. And, as they say, 'the rest is history'.

In life, many things can cause discouragement, causing us to lose heart, courage, and perspective. Maybe this could be an unforeseen circumstance, work, family, pressure and stress, a personal failure, a financial setback, an uncertain future or a sudden crisis. Sometimes overtiredness, illness, or a hurtful word or action from a friend or work colleague can set us back.

I remember going through a difficult and discouraging period in my own ministry; I was burnt out and felt washed up, and so took the decision to leave the ministry to go into business. Feeling depressed and dejected, Deb took me to Windsor Great Park on a sunny Saturday. At the top of the park is a huge statue of a horse and rider, and you can look all the way down a long avenue of trees to Windsor Castle. I was tired, worn out, beaten and defeated. We sat on the grass in the shadow of the horse and rider, and after a while I lay down closed my eyes, struggling with my own thoughts and a deep sense of failure and dejection.

After a while, I heard voices of children playing nearby. Suddenly they began to sing a worship song I recognized, 'Ah Lord God, thou hast made the heavens and the earth by thy great power, nothing, nothing absolutely nothing, nothing is too difficult for thee. O great and mighty God, Great in power and mighty in deed, Nothing, nothing, absolutely nothing, Nothing is too difficult for Thee.' [6] They didn't just sing it once, like most small children do they sang it over and over again; it washed over my soul and I wept before God. After a while, I composed myself, got up off the grass to look for the children, but by then they were gone. Were they angels? No, they were small children; Deb saw them. They were two little boys singing words of consolation and encouragement that touched a dejected, defeated, forlorn preacher. That day those two little boys became my jump leads.

These boys never knew they'd rescued a broken preacher from the brink of spiritual despair. As we left the park, I heard myself quietly beginning to sing, 'Ah Lord God, thou hast made the heavens and the earth by thy great power, nothing, nothing absolutely nothing, nothing is impossible to you'. That day, unintentionally, just through the expression of their daily lives, the jump leads of consolation and encouragement were connected to the depleted, dead batteries in my spirit, giving strength, hope and stability. You see, you may never know the impact you make through the expression of your life.

## Think about it

As well as unintentional encouragement through the way we live our lives, we should consider and give attention to how we can intentionally encourage others. The Amplified Bible, Classic Edition says, 'let us consider *and* give attentive, continuous care to watching over one another, studying how we may stir up (stimulate and incite) to love *and* helpful deeds *and* noble activities' (Heb. 10:24). This is *paraclesis* at work. It doesn't just happen by chance but by intentionally and thoughtfully thinking through ways we can jump start someone else's journey, helping them to make a fresh start. We can be the one who can lift them up and set them on their way again. 'Two are better than one, because they have a good return for their labour' (Eccl. 4:9, NIV). That's the power of consolation and encouragement.

Here are some ideas for how to console and encourage others:

### Be willing to be a jump lead

Moving out of our own comfort zone is the first challenge. Encouragement begins by making the effort to connect. Looking beyond our own circumstances and moving towards others from where we are to where they are, 'coming alongside'.

### Develop your awareness of other people's struggles

Learning to recognise and read the signals of discouragement people send out. Their tone of voice, facial expressions, language, demeanour and attitude. They are like puffs of smoke, often with a volcano simmering underneath, waiting to erupt.

### Become a giver, not a getter

Being willing to give encouragement rather than receiving or looking for it. Acts 20:35 says, 'It is more blessed to give than to receive'. We can't truly encourage unless we are prepared to do it expecting nothing in return, with no sense of what might be in it for us.

### Be a good listener

Attentive listening is an expression of loving. Most of us are better talkers than listeners, but, as the quip goes, God has given us two ears and one mouth so that we can listen twice as much as we talk. One of the most encouraging things we can do is to take time to attentively listen.

### Use positive uplifting and affirming words

Words are powerful, they can bless or blister, build up or tear down, heal or hurt, soothe or sear. Encouragers use words of affirmation and validation, focusing on what is positive and possible, endorsing the potential and good they see in others.

### Engage in acts of kindness

We can all make a phone call, drop a note, send an email, pay a visit, post a card, send some flowers, give some cash, not now and again but regularly until the hard time has passed. You can make someone's heart smile. The Scottish theologian John Watson said, 'Be kind, everyone you meet is fighting a hard battle.'[7] We all face weekly struggles and all need consolation and encouragement. The world is full of discouragers! People need to be encouraged, not only because of bad things that happen, but because it can sometimes feel like few good things happen. Encouragers are people it's good to be around; they're uplifting! A breath of fresh air and encouragement is contagious … and you never know who needs it.

## CHAPTER 3

# 'You're not right for the part'

'So speak encouraging [*parakaleo*] words to one another. Build up hope so you'll all be together in this, no one left out, no one left behind. I know you're already doing this; just keep on doing it.' (1 Thess. 5:11, MSG)

People easily get discouraged. If we're honest, every one of us has felt discouraged at one time or another on the journey of life. Discouragement is an issue we all grapple with in a variety of forms. Let's be clear, sometimes life just isn't fair. If left to its own devices, discouragement can drag us down to the depths of depression. A set of circumstances triggers a set of emotions, which in turn triggers a set of reactions. You'll hear discouraged people say things like, 'Things are hopeless', 'They'll never change', 'What's the use of trying?' and 'I give up'. In a world such as ours, we can all be easily discouraged and dispirited. That's why the encouragement facet of the *paraclesis* diamond is so important. The question is: Why do people get discouraged?

## The stage of life is set

One day, a discouraged Charlie Brown was talking to his friend Linus about the pervasive sense of inadequacy he feels all the time. Charlie moaned, 'You see, Linus, it goes all the way back to the beginning. The moment I was born and set foot on the stage of life, they took one look at me and said, "You're not right for the part."'[1]

The world can be a discouraging and hurtful place. The rejection that the character of Charlie Brown summarises is deeply dispiriting. I think he could have been speaking for us all; we all get discouraged with ourselves at times. Discouragement is a thief that robs us of our vitality, joy, peace, and purpose, bringing with it its closest pals: insecurity, inadequacy, hopelessness, despair, self-pity, depression and doubt. Orison Swett Marden said, 'Discouragement, fear, doubt, lack of self-confidence, are the germs which have killed the prosperity and happiness of tens of thousands of people.'[2]

Like Charlie Brown, our own sense of insecurity, inadequacy and discouragement can hold us back. We think we're just 'not right for the part'. We feel we're just not cut out to play the role the stage of life has carved out for us. Where does this come from? I think Charlie Brown is onto something when he says, 'You see, Linus, it goes all the way back to the beginning.' One of the deeply discouraging things that comes early in life is rejection. It's a basic fear of the human heart from which we never seem to escape. At the core of our beings is a deep-seated longing for acceptance and affirmation, accompanied by a fear that who we are and what we do won't be acceptable. It can be easy for us to view everything that goes against us negatively in life as a personal rejection, and when we do we can feel 'not right for the part'.

Many years ago a Jesuit Priest and professor of theology and psychology, John Powell, wrote a book titled *Why Am I Afraid to Tell You Who I Am?*. His book comes to the conclusion, 'I am afraid to tell you who I am because you might not like me, and that is all I have to give you.'[3] At the heart of our humanness is an inherent fear that if we're seen and known as we are, we won't be liked and accepted. I heard about a lady who committed suicide and when they found her, she was clutching a note in her hand. When they uncrumpled the note it read, 'They said …' but the statement was left unfinished. I wonder what they said that drove her from discouragement to despair, that made her feel she was 'not right for the part'. Overt and covert rejection experienced in our relationships with others can be devastating, and can turn to a destructive force in our personalities.

Some years ago, a group of psychologists met to discuss what they considered to be important for healthy emotional and psychological development. They came to the conclusion that if a child doesn't regularly receive encouragement and affirmation when growing up, they will be deprived of the necessary emotional and psychological nurture necessary to become a healthy, wholesome personality in adult life. They concluded that such a child grows up feeling discouraged with themselves, developing behaviour patterns to compensate for their feelings of discouragement, rejection, insecurity and inadequacy. I think this is what Charlie Brown is alluding to. Although undoubtedly there is much truth in this analysis, it's worth asking the question: Is there a deeper cause of discouragement, insecurity and inadequacy?

## Back to the beginning

As it was sung in *The Sound of Music*, 'Let's start at the very beginning, A very good place to start.' To find the genesis of discouragement and rejection we must commence at the book of beginnings, Genesis, the root of humanity. It began in a garden. Adam and Eve had an idyllic life, enjoying unclouded communion with God, and in the cool of the day – the evening – He came down alongside, walking and talking with them. In God's presence they experienced unconditional acceptance, unlimited, joyous love and complete openness, accepted and loved for who they were. 'And they were both naked, the man and his wife, and were not ashamed' (Gen. 2:25). Their acceptability was not based on dress code, performance levels, status symbols or their appearance. Approval did not depend on them putting their best foot forward. They enjoyed full approval in the security of God's presence, with nothing to fear.

It all changed when they went missing one evening and couldn't be found. They were hiding and cowering in the bushes, so God called out to Adam, 'Where *are* you?' (Gen. 3:9). Listen to Adam's response, 'I heard your voice in the garden, and I was afraid because I was naked; and I hid myself' (v10). In those words we find the roots of insecurity, the real heart of discouragement, inadequacy and fear of unacceptability. Adam left a legacy we've all come to inherit. As the psychologists suggest, these innate fears are further compounded through life experience, in childhood, teens and early adulthood where we experience the pain, hurt, and humiliation of rejection at the hands of others.

## Hide and seek

Suddenly aware of their nakedness, Adam and Eve feel exposed and vulnerable. Not just their physical nudity, they'd been naked and unashamed, now their hearts are exposed and they're deeply afraid. They no longer feel acceptable, secure or adequate, so they hide, thinking they can cover their feelings up, first with fig leaves, then in the bushes. God calls out, 'Where *are* you?' not because He'd lost Adam but because He wanted to call him out from hiding. This was the very first game of hide-and-seek, and someone has said that man has been trying to hide ever since. Like Adam, we search for ways to cover up and dress up our feelings, to protect ourselves from exposure and risk of further rejection.

In God's presence they'd known unqualified acceptance, unconditional love and unclouded communion. Now they found themselves on the outside of the garden. The security they'd experienced in relationship with God in the garden now became a deep issue of insecurity in the soul. The attributes of life found in God suddenly turned to deep needs, innermost longings for acceptance, security and value. And from that day to this, man has been searching for ways to meet these deep needs and longings, and to cover up and hide his deep feelings of insecurity. You see, these are not simply psychological needs as the group of psychologists found, but deep spiritual needs.

## Playing it safe

To insulate ourselves from the pain and hurt of rejection, we learn to develop subtle self-protective strategies, building self-defensive barriers, and shielding walls to safeguard against exposure and rejection. We learn ways of functioning, patterns of behaviours and lifestyles we think will make us appear more acceptable, and less inadequate. As a result, the human personality becomes adept at finding ways to relate to people with our real self hidden from view. We develop ways to compensate; we become, people pleasers, attention seekers, workaholics, perfectionists, clowns, and victims, experts in the art of camouflage. It's a journey we've all experienced. The fear of exposure is so strong we learn to hide behind masks.

An old aphorism says: We are not what we think we are, we are not even what others think we are, we are what we think others think we are. There's a lot of truth in this statement. Each of us evaluates what we believe others think about us then play that prescribed role. The fear of rejection becomes a hidden agenda of the human condition and a powerful driver in the human personality. We become fearful of expressing and admitting our deep struggles, afraid of unacceptability and rejection, so we cover up. Our number one fear is rejection and our number one need is acceptance. This is a hugely discouraging and debilitating way to live.

## Snooker-table churches

Because of our sense of inadequacy we learn to hide in all kinds of places, including the church. I heard of a church who were so concerned about the lack of being open, honest and real with each other, hiding behind masks, that the pastor put a sign up in the foyer near the coat pegs either side of the entrance door. One side said, 'Please hang your coats and hats here', and on the other side it said, 'Please leave your masks here'. Someone has described these kinds of churches as snooker-table churches. Where we come to church, out from our little pockets and bounce off each other like balls on a snooker table – click, click – before disappearing back into our pockets again.

We often hide behind clichés making passing enquiries like, 'How are you?', and with their struggles people answer, 'Just fine', when really they're hurting. 'How's your family?' ... 'Great, thanks', when their family is really struggling. 'Where are you going?' ... 'Not too far'. 'I like your dress' ... 'I like yours too, very nice, suits you.' Familiar statements that roll off the end our tongue without thinking. We're taken somewhat by surprise if the other person starts answering in detail, because we aren't really concerned about their struggles. Then we return home, back into our pockets and after a week come out and go through the exercise all over again. Very rarely do people genuinely come alongside others, displaying real, open, honest *paraclesis*, in these kinds of churches.

There's a longing in the human heart to be accepted, affirmed and encouraged. Why? Because God made us that way: to feel accepted, secure and valued. He's called us into a community of faith that should provide acceptance, encouragement, affirmation and value, providing a safe environment where people can take off their masks without fear of condemnation and rejection, to be able to come out from the barriers they have built up over many years.

## Layer-to-layer fellowship

When we only relate to each other from behind our masks and barriers we create a superficial, shallow level of fellowship that is guarded and defensive. We experience layer-to-layer fellowship with a phoney façade of spirituality. That is to say that we relate only on the surface of our lives, to what we see outwardly, top layer to top layer. We attempt to develop a rapport with each other from behind our defensive guarded positions.

Following my theological training, I did chaplaincy work for a short time in a prison in the American Midwest. It was always sad when visiting time came once a month to see loved ones trying to touch hands through the glass pane separating them. But saddest of all, after an all too short visiting time, was to see them try and kiss each other through a pane of toughened bullet-proof glass. Someone has said that church can be like two lovers trying to kiss through a pane of glass.

Often we have not created the safe, caring *Paraclesis* environment where people feel they can share their deepest struggles for fear of condemnation. Instead of acceptance and understanding they feel threatened by exposure and condemnation. They reason, 'I am afraid that you are going judge me, expose me, then criticise and condemn me, so I will not allow myself to be vulnerable to that risk.' They're afraid to express their deep struggles, for fear of unacceptability. To be seen as being unspiritual, even sinful or backslidden.

The very place that ought to provide the safe environment to share our deepest fears and inner struggles often fails us. Church can be a discouraging place. Remember the old song, 'Home, home on the range, where the deer and the antelope play, where seldom is heard a discouraging word and the skies are not cloudy all day.' [4] Maybe in some churches the line would read, 'where never is heard an encouraging word'. One person said their biggest discouragements came from Christian friends. Even the pastor isn't exempt.

Several years ago I preached a message entitled 'The Enlarged Heart' to the Sunday morning congregation, announcing that my message the following week would be 'The Favour of God'. Ironically, I woke up on the Monday morning to begin my preparation, and promptly suffered a severe heart attack. Thank God I survived, but it was many months of recovering before I entered the pulpit again to preach on The Favour of God from a completely different perspective. I was so happy and excited to be back in the pulpit that

I think it must have been reflected in my preaching. Shaking hands at the door at the close of the service, an elderly lady shook my hand and said, 'Pastor Trevor, if you preach like that, no wonder you get heart attacks!' Rick Warren empathises when he says, 'Do you know how often I have wanted to quit being pastor of Saddleback Church? Every Monday morning!'[5]

## Stop hiding

Openness and honesty is at the heart of authenticity and integrity. It means being real, a willingness to be transparent and vulnerable with others. Where we feel secure and accepted enough to share with someone the deepest fears, doubts, hurts, and struggles of our soul. We feel understood and accepted, and are willing to open ourselves to each other, when we recognize someone accepts and understands us who has walked the pathway of struggle themselves. When someone is willing to come alongside to be there for us to encourage and affirm us.

The very thing we may have hidden could well be the solution to someone else's struggle. God can use those very struggles in the life of someone else. You see, the only place God can truly meet us is at the place of honesty. Psalm 51:6 says, 'Behold, you desire truth in the inward parts'. The Contemporary English Version puts it as, 'But you want complete honesty'. And the place for honesty is the cross, where, when I am honest with God and confess my sin and failure, I receive acceptance and forgiveness. Paul, writing to the Ephesians, said, 'no more lies, no more pretence. Tell your neighbour the truth. In Christ's body we're all connected to each other' (Eph. 4:25, MSG).

It is our willingness to remove the masks we wear, let down the barriers, take down the walls we've built, revealing our true selves, that opens the door. It is not easy, because of our stubborn commitment to self-protection and wanting to hide from reality. But you see, in God's purposes, it is more important that we're honest than appearing to be successful by hiding behind a façade and veneer of respectability.

The sad fact is that usually beneath the confident outward appearance, are lonely, insecure people with deep needs. God wants to call us out of our hiding, to get alongside others. 'Coming alongside' means being willing to share something of yourself, the real you. Not a sugar-coated version. It's time to stop hiding from each other in church, time for 'coming alongside', opening up to each other and getting real. As Clyde Narramore said, 'Everyone is worth understanding.' [6]

## An open-hearted community

When Adam stepped outside the garden it truly was paradise lost. The extension of heaven on earth, the garden of Eden closed its gates and shut down once and for all. There was no way back in. Adam learned when love flows out, fear flows in. The message of the gospel is: what was lost in Adam has been restored in Christ – not only at the cross through salvation from sin, but in the context of Christian community, the family of God. A new community of grace and truth, where acceptance, belonging, security and value are the order of the day. Where the antidote of rejection, inadequacy and discouragement is encouragement, affirmation and validation. Where people are enabled to step out from behind their barriers, and climb over their walls. A community of the open heart, of love and care, where people 'come alongside', drawing others out from underneath their layers to experience the warmth and reassurance of God's love and grace. When love flows in, fear will flow out. 'There is no fear in love, but perfect love casts out fear' (1 John 4:18).

If we are to be those who 'come alongside', fulfilling the *paraclesis* role, there must be a willingness to remove our own masks, allowing ourselves to be vulnerable. We need to first find ourselves, looking within with honesty and integrity, coming out from our own hiding places. If we have unresolved issues from the past, we must confront them and be released through truth and grace. So often this prevents us reaching out and 'coming alongside' others. Sometimes the risk of rejection and misunderstanding just seems too great. So rather than take the risk, like Adam we learn to take cover and hide our true selves.

Being open hearted to someone is one of the biggest testaments we can show of our care, trust, encouragement and love towards others. 'By opening up to others, you'll prompt people to open up with God, this generous Father in heaven' (Matt 5:16, MSG).

'Coming alongside' is to be accepting, understanding and supportive of others who are struggling. Creating an environment where people feel they belong and are valued and accepted for who they are; that God's gracious acceptance of them in Christ is reflected by their unqualified acceptance into His family, warts and all. Everyone should see themselves accepted unreservedly by God embracing their new reality, 'accepted in the Beloved' (Eph. 1:6).

'This is how we've come to understand and experience love: Christ sacrificed his life for us. This is why we ought to live sacrificially for our fellow believers, and not just be out for ourselves. If you see some brother or sister in need and have the means to do something about it but turn a cold shoulder and do nothing, what happens to God's love? It disappears. And you made it disappear. My dear children, let's not just talk about love; let's practice real love' (1 John 3:16–18, MSG). I guess the question is: How would someone like Charlie Brown feel in your church?

## CHAPTER 4

# Front-door, back-door syndrome

'Let us be concerned for one another, to help one another to show love and to do good. Let us not give up the habit of meeting together, as some are doing. Instead, let us encourage [*parakaleo*] one another' (Heb. 10:24–25, GNT)

I sat at my desk one day and took a call from a businessman, who was passing through London Heathrow Airport from the USA and was was in deep trouble. Someone had given him my name and phone number, telling him I could be of help. When I arrived at his hotel room on the edge of the airport he poured out to me the problems of his life. At the conclusion of a couple of hours with him, I suggested that when he returned from his business trip, he connect to a local church.

'Well', he said, 'that's another part of the problem. Someone else told me the same thing, and I did just that. But after three weeks of attending it was clear the church was in the middle of a major fight, and although I was new, people were trying to pull me in different directions. After a few weeks I'd had enough and never returned.'

I drove back from the airport to my office saddened and heavy-hearted. We work so hard to get people into church, but often they find the church isn't the caring community they're expecting.

## Something better to offer

There's no question we have a responsibility to reach out to all who find themselves in need. However, sometimes the focus on active evangelistic outreach to the non-churched community can be such that we fail to recognise the immediate needs of those among us. Many churches suffer from front-door, back-door syndrome, so busy concentrating on getting people through the front door, they fail to recognise those rapidly slipping through the back door. Or, as in the case of the man I met at the airport, a revolving door syndrome. As soon as people come in they see we don't really know how to care for each other, never mind care for them, and they leave the same way they came in.

In asking people over many years why they left a particular church the vast majority have told me it was because they felt uncared for, unaccepted and undervalued. My experience is that most don't leave because of style, doctrine, practice, music, leadership issues, or personality clashes. Some do, of course, but most leave because they don't find a sense of belonging or community there. They don't feel valued and cared for.

How sad. There's a huge difference between attending and belonging. How can we say we care for sinners if we don't care for those who are part of the family of God? 'When we have the opportunity to help anyone, we should do it. But we should give special attention to those who are in the family of believers' (Gal. 6:10, NCV).

I heard of a Christian visiting a doctors' surgery who invited the receptionist to an evangelistic event at their church. She politely declined, saying, 'You know, so many from your church visit here each week suffering with stress. When you have something better to offer, I'll think about coming.' How sad is that? When I visited my surgery recently I saw emotional and mental health workshops offered on the notice board with times and dates, for stress, anxiety, anger, low self-esteem, frustration, and low moods. Surely if our message is for real we should be experts in the Church on these life issues, not because we're causing them but because we're solving them. As the community of grace this should be our culture. However, when we can't take care of our own, people turn to secular agencies for the help the Church fails to provide.

## A 'coming alongside' culture

The Church is called to be a caring community, a 'coming alongside' community. 'Let us be concerned for one another, to help one another to show love and to do good. Let us not give up the habit of meeting together, as some are doing. Instead, let us encourage [*parakaleo*] one another' (Heb. 10:24–25, GNT). The writer of Hebrews says we should continue coming together, not just to hold meetings, but to get alongside, encourage, support and help each other. The Greek word for 'habit' is 'ethos', meaning 'custom' or 'culture'. Some had withdrawn, walked away, rejected and forsaken the Church like the businessman I met at Heathrow airport. They suffered from the front-door, back-door syndrome. To those remaining, the writer is saying not to let more walk away, but instead create and maintain a *paraclesis ethos*.

Culture doesn't just happen by chance; it is created. Every church and family creates its culture by design or default. 'Culture' is an agricultural word meaning the kind of nutrients and soil that enable something to grow and flourish. A rose doesn't grow well in sand. It needs a culture of rich, loamy soil to enable its fragrance, colour, and beauty to bloom.

Some churches become so focused on their vision and projects that they neglect to nurture a caring culture. Projects, programmes and theological niceties take precedence over people. They doggedly pursue them and in the process leave casualties by the wayside. However, when we take time to create a caring culture, vision crystalises, mission becomes more focused and truth comes to life. Culture always sets context.

So we need to consider how God can use us in 'coming alongside' those who are struggling on their own journey through life.

The Christian community is uniquely designed to care. God has called us to 'be' Church, not to 'do' Church. We're a Body, not a club or organisation, a living organism with life and vitality. 'In Christ's body we're all connected to each other' (Eph. 4:25, MSG). Once we become members in Christ's Body we are part of one another, 'so we, *being* many, are one body in Christ, and individually members of one another' (Rom. 12:5). *Paraclesis* – 'coming alongside others' – isn't only a ministry for pastors on Sundays but for every believer; not just the few, it's everyone's responsibility. A caring culture is about taking responsibility for each other. No one in the Body of Christ should have to face something alone. 'But if we say we love God and don't love each other, we are liars. We cannot see God. So how can we love God, if we don't love the people we can see?' (1 John 4:20, CEV).

## A warm embrace

After all, what's the purpose of coming to church? To hear a sermon, sing, give tithes and offerings, worship, raise our hands, get caught up in all the church activity? They're part of it, but every Sunday is an opportunity to meaningfully come alongside others, a significant time to make an impact on each other, to be a community of care.

'Right now, therefore, every time we get the chance, let us work for the benefit of all, starting with the people closest to us in the community of faith' (Gal. 6:10, MSG). When we come together, we need to intentionally look out for people to get alongside. Even before coming to church we need to think about it, about where we sit, who we should sit next to, trying to not sit in the same seat every service. Who we sit next to is important to them and important to God, so that at the service close we can open up, share and meaningfully engage with each other rather than simply passing like ships in the night. It's good to turn to the person next to us and ask about their week, and, if appropriate, pray with each other. Then add them to your 'bake a cake' list, your prayer list, your 'let's text' list, your 'let's send a note' list, so that during the week the culture we share as we gather together continues. Hebrews says, don't neglect *paraclesis*, but continue it. Not now and again or occasionally, monthly or weekly, but regularly, on-going, supporting, affirming, valuing, and strengthening. 'So encourage [*parakaleo*] each other to build each other up' (1 Thess. 5:11, TLB).

God is in the business of 'coming alongside' and has called us to the business of 'coming alongside others' in the community of faith. 'Bear one another's burdens, and so fulfil the law of Christ' (Gal. 6:2). One of Aesop's Fables tells of a dispute between the sun and the wind as to who was strongest. A traveller was journeying in a heavy overcoat. 'Watch me', said the wind as he blew strong and hard, but the traveller wrapped his coat around him more tightly. The harsh northerly winds made him feel cold, lonely and isolated. The harsh, cold, unforgiving blast of the winds of criticism, judgment and condemnation cause us to close in.

But the bright sun came out with his welcoming warmth, heat and light. 'Watch me', he said, as he shone upon the weary traveller. Soon the traveller wanted to take off his cumbersome, heavy coat and bask in the warm glow of the sun's presence. Now he walked freely and openly with the sun on his back.

That's how the culture of our churches should be, coming alongside with a warm, open spirit, hearts open to each other. People thrive in a culture of the warm, welcoming embrace of knowing they belong, are accepted, affirmed, approved and valued. People seek places where people believe in them, where they know people genuinely have their best interests at heart.

## The highest possible good

Jesus commands such a culture of support and care at the deepest level. 'A new commandment I give to you, that you love one another; as I have loved you' (John 13:34). This isn't an option or suggestion, or even a choice. It's the eleventh commandment; the gold standard

Jesus sets for the culture of His new community. So important was this commandment that Jesus repeats it again in John 15:12–13: 'This is my commandment, that you love one another as I have loved you', adding a strong rider, 'Greater love has no one than this, than to lay down one's life for his friends.'

When I first became a Christian I struggled to understand the concept of God's love. I understood teenage love, parental love, sibling love; but in my newfound Christian world, God's love seemed hard to define. Someone suggested I needed to understand the four different Greek words for love, so I read C.S. Lewis's *The Four Loves*. These are: *storge*, family and filial bond; *eros*, the sexual bond; *phileo*, a friendship bond; and *agape*, the bonds of God's love, the Christian virtue. But as a new Christian, I found this confusing. It seemed to me that *agape* was an airy-fairy spiritualised concept. Some time later I came across a quote of Charles Finney, an old-time American evangelist, who helped me begin to grasp it. He gave a very practical definition. He said, 'love is bringing about the highest possible good in another individual's life.'[1] Thomas Aquinas put it, *agape* is 'to will the good of another.'[2]

Suddenly I had a handle on what God's love looked like. I dropped it into a couple of scriptures. John 3:16, 'For God so loved the world'. I read it as, 'For God so wanted to bring about the highest possible good for mankind that He sent His only Son'. He wanted the best, so He gave the best. Revelation 3:19 says, 'As many as I love, I rebuke'. I read it as, 'Those who I want to bring about the highest possible good I discipline, not out of anger, frustration or punishment, but because I want the best for them and what I see them doing is not in their own best interest, so I need to correct them for their own good'. 1 Thessalonians 5:15 (MSG) puts it, 'Look for the best in each other, and always do your best to bring it out.'

That's the goal, a culture that desires and works towards God's best for each other. 'If we have all we need and see one of our own people in need, we must have pity on that person, or else we cannot say we love God. Children, you show love for others by truly helping them, and not merely by talking about it' (1 John 3:17–18, CEV).

## Receiving and giving love

Some people spend all their time worrying about how much they love God, and it never seems enough. But they have it backwards. We won't ever know how to love God and others until we understand how much God loves us! 'In this is love, not that we loved God, but that He loved us' (1 John 4:10).

Some have grown up under the cloud that we should love God more. But the problem is not that we don't love God enough, but that we don't know how much He loves us. God is not mad at us, but mad *about* us. In fact, He's head over heels in love with us. We don't have to earn His love. That's religion. He does not love us because of what we do or don't do, but simply because He's chosen to set His love upon us. That's the message of the gospel. His love is not about our performance or status or putting our best foot forward. In fact, if we went to sleep for a year and did nothing, God would love us just the same when we woke up. It's about the provision of His love for us in Jesus.

Pastor Bruce Larson says he asked a successful pastor what his secret was. 'Simple', he said, 'I just tell people who they are – chosen by God, his children, his priests. I don't shame them for what they're not; I tell them who they are.'[3]

When we know how much God loves us, our love responds to Him, and flows out towards others. The more we realise how much God loves us, warts and all, the easier it is for us to love people, especially when they aren't being very lovable. His love for us comes first, and in the strength of that love we are empowered to love others, even when we think it's impossible. We can't manufacture His love, only receive it.

Dr Karl Stern, a neurologist and psychologist, said that in his observation of human behaviour over many years, he believed there are two fundamental needs. In his view, if these two needs could be met, all psychological problems and emotional disturbance could be resolved. He said they are the need to receive love, and the need to give love.[4]

When we know how to receive love we feel accepted, affirmed, valued, a sense of belonging, and find purpose in loving as we have been loved. Isn't this what our *paraclesis* verses say in 2 Corinthians 1:3–4? As God's love 'comes alongside' us and we receive and embrace it, He then brings us alongside others to give that love to them. It's love that comes alongside. Jesus said, 'Love each other in the same way I have loved you' (John 15:12, NLT). To love as I have been loved is to value others as I am valued, to accept others as I have been accepted, to affirm others as I have been affirmed, to forgive others as I have been forgiven. People flourish in a culture of acceptance, affirmation and value, where they feel worthwhile and belong.

The term 'one another' means I belong, I'm loved, I'm valued, I'm secure. This is what happens when we worship. As we receive God's love upon us, our hearts respond by expressing our love for Him – it's reciprocal. Why do we take bread and wine? To celebrate sacrifice, yes, but also to celebrate and receive the love of God in Jesus. This is the true culture of love; receiving and giving love; the 'coming alongside' community at its best.

## The expression of authentic culture

Jesus said, 'everyone will know that you are my disciples, if you have love *and* unselfish concern for one another' (John 13:35, AMP). Jesus didn't say, 'you'll know they're my disciples by their great vision, their noble projects, the size of their congregation, their extensive programmes or their evangelistic efforts'. The discipleship test is none of these things. Jesus didn't even say, 'men will know you're my disciples by the love you have for me'. Proof of discipleship is not our love for Jesus but the expression of our love and care for each other.

The litmus paper test of being followers of Jesus is our culture of care. That is, how we treat one another. The *paraclesis* culture. He was saying not to look at what they're doing by their activity, industry, religious rituals and services, or saying with their religious clichés and pious language, but look at the culture, look at who they are together to see if they're genuine, authentic, by their level of deep care for each other. The gospel of Jesus Christ isn't only about salvation from sin, but that through the cross we're brought into God's family, where the deepest longings and needs of the human heart can be fully met through Christ in the context of Christian community.

At the centre of a 'coming alongside' culture is a compassionate heart. Compassion moves us to engage with others. Compassion in the Greek language originates from the word for the kidneys or bowels. It's a vivid word, meaning to be gripped in the pit of your stomach, or as we say, a 'gut feeling'. Compassion moves us inwardly, and engages us outwardly. Paul said, 'For the love of Christ compels us' (2 Cor. 5:14), which means it motivates, monopolises, moves, grips, consumes and controls us.

*The Message* puts it, 'Christ's love has moved me to such extremes. His love has the first and last word in everything we do'. If a friend's child is sick we genuinely show pity and sympathy, but when our own child is sick we would willingly change places with them. We're desperate to be alongside, to be there for them, easing their pain and discomfort. Compassion feels something, engages with something, and grips us to do whatever we can.

Wherever we follow Jesus' journey, the Gospel writers record that He was moved with compassion. It doesn't say He had compassion but was 'moved with compassion'. It is a verb, not a noun. Compassion always moves us to get involved. He saw the need, came alongside, engaged with people and a miracle happened. Whether it was the widow of Nain whose son was raised to life, Bartimaeus, a blind man in Jericho whose sight was restored, a leper healed in Galilee, Lazarus at Bethany or the miracle of the loaves and fishes, it says Jesus was *moved* with compassion.

## Compassion deficit disorder

The feeding of the 5,000 is hugely significant because it's the only miracle performed by Jesus recorded by all four gospel writers. As well as those four accounts there are two further accounts of feeding 4,000. Jesus journeys with His disciples across the lake to a hillside. Without warning, a great multitude follow them round the lake. Suddenly their quiet retreat is gatecrashed and hijacked by a huge crowd of 5,000 men, plus women and children. Usually there are more women and children in church than men, so to my reckoning there could have been at least 15,000. Wouldn't you be pleased if 15,000 people showed up for church one Sunday morning? These disciples weren't. The vast crowd were hungry and needed feeding, but the disciples hadn't yet learned the culture of care. The needy crowd were an intrusion, disrupting their holy huddle with Jesus. They said 'Lord, send them away, they can find their own food. Tell them to go the villages and surrounding countryside to eat'.

Jesus, 'moved with compassion', saw the crowd not as hungry, tired, problem people, but as 'sheep having no shepherd' (Matt. 9:36); 'lost sheep of the house of Israel' (Matt. 15:24). They didn't belong even in their own land, oppressed and suppressed by Rome. Jesus was not simply a man on a mission or a man engaged in a project, but a man moved with compassion. It was the compassion of Christ that brought about the miracle provision of the loaves and fishes for this hungry multitude.

Where there is compassion, miracles happen, it is the seedbed of the miraculous, but these disciples suffered from compassion deficit disorder. They were not yet a 'coming alongside' community, but a 'sending away' community with a front-door, back-door mentality. The culture of care with a compassionate heart is the watermark of a 'coming alongside' community that throws its front door widely open, so when the non-churched come in they feel and see that love. In a church with such a core culture, the back door will remain firmly closed.

## CHAPTER 5

# Nothing is lost or wasted

'I'm working hard to *comfort* [*parakaleo*] *and* encourage them so *that they will be knit together* – that many hearts would become one through His love. ... Now that you have welcomed the Anointed One, Jesus the Lord, into your lives, continue to journey with Him *and allow Him to shape your lives.*' (Col. 2:2,6, TV)

Forrest Gump said, 'Momma always said, "Life is like a box of chocolates, you never know what you're gonna get."'[1] As Forrest knew, the road of life is never straight. It has ups and downs, twists and turns, bumps and potholes, valleys and rocky places. If we think we can avoid struggle and hard times, we're misguided. As the saying goes, 'stuff happens'. Job lamented, 'man is born to trouble, As sparks fly upward' (Job 5:7). Like Forrest, none of us are exempt from things life has a habit of throwing at us, but as he found, half the battle is having others there for us. As the old adage says, 'a burden shared is a burden halved'.

*Paraclesis* is turning up and being there for someone in times of trouble – coming alongside – and journeying is walking beside them as a fellow traveller. It's good to have those close at hand who are understanding, supportive, non-judgmental, and caring; who are just willing to be there, helping us get through the challenges of the moment.

We've all travelled different life journeys but we never know the road another person has walked until we walk beside them. Everyone needs a fellow traveller, both in good and bad times. 'He brings us alongside someone else who is going through hard times' (2 Cor. 1:3, MSG). We find strength and courage to face reality as someone walks beside us. 'It's better to have a partner than go it alone ... if one falls down, the other helps, But if there's no one to help, tough!' (Eccl. 4:9–10, MSG).

## Life is a journey

It's been well said, 'The journey is the truest metaphor of human life.' It's a central theme of Scripture. Jesus continually journeyed throughout the Gospels, from Bethlehem to Jerusalem, Jericho to Capernaum, Jordan to Galilee. In fact, the Gospels are mainly a narrative of Jesus journeying with the twelve. Luke 8:1 says, 'He went through every city and village …. And the twelve *were* with Him'. Wherever we follow Him, He's engaging with people, stopping and getting alongside them as they open their lives to Him: Nicodemus the Pharisee, a seeking soul in Jerusalem, Zacchaeus the chief tax collector in Jericho, a blind man by the pool of Siloam, publicans at a meal table in Capernaum, ten lepers in Samaria, a hungry multitude on a hillside in Galilee.

Early believers called themselves followers of the Way. It meant more than following the teachings of Jesus, but a commitment to journeying in life as He did. Peter reiterates this, describing early Christians as 'pilgrims' (1 Pet. 2:11). In classic seventeenth-century Christian literature, John Bunyan's *The Pilgrim's Progress* came to epitomise the Christian life. For centuries it ranked just behind the King James Bible as the most important book in Protestant households. It's an allegory of a Christian traveller on the journey of life.

Everyone experiences difficult days and 'hard times'. Life is a full contact game of hard knocks. Some translations say 'troubles' (NIV), 'tribulation' or 'travail' (KJV). They're all the same Greek word *thlipsis*, used by Jesus when He said: 'In this world you will have trouble' (John 16:33, NIV). The meaning is: squeezing, pressure, pressing together, struggle, stress. Jesus uses the word again when talking about the 'travail' (struggle) of a woman in childbirth in John 16:21 (KJV), that is, the cramping, squeezing, pushing, and after the struggle, the joy of birth. It's interesting the word 'travel' comes from 'travail' (old French, *travailler*), meaning to struggle and toil through an arduous and difficult journey.

Struggle is a part of life, so it's okay to struggle. When we can reach out to others for support we can learn to struggle well together. Paul says, 'Gently encourage the stragglers, and reach out for the exhausted, pulling them to their feet. Be patient with each person, attentive to individual needs' (1 Thess. 5:14, MSG). The origin of struggle comes from stumbling and getting back on our feet. We've all seen a small child struggling to walk. They say a child stumbles and falls 300–400 times before finally walking by himself; that each time the child stumbles, he walks a little further. If a parent wasn't there, pulling them to their feet, there'd be little hope of the child getting back up to get going again by themselves.

Journeying is being right there in the stumblings and struggles of life, pulling someone to their feet again. Alex Elle said, 'I am thankful for my struggle because without it I wouldn't have stumbled across my strength'.[2]

## A door of hope

Hosea 2:15 says, 'I will give ... the Valley of Achor [trouble] as a door of hope'. *Paraclesis* is travelling with someone through their valley of trouble, being the door of hope on someone's journey. Our very presence is a door of hope that help will come from God. We are that help from God. 'For indeed, when we came to Macedonia, our bodies had no rest, but we were troubled on every side. Outside *were* conflicts, inside *were* fears.

Nevertheless God, who comforts [*parakleo*] the downcast, comforted [*parakleo*] us by the coming of Titus' (2 Cor. 7:5–6).

The psalmist David said, 'Even when I walk through the darkest valley, I fear no danger because you are with me' (Psa. 23:4, CEB). This is the journey psalm – it begins, 'The LORD *is* my shepherd', the shepherd guiding and journeying with him. An old Zambian proverb says: 'When you run alone, you run fast. But when you run together, you run far.'[3]

'Your life is a journey you must travel with a deep consciousness of God' (1 Pet. 1:18, MSG). When we find ourselves in the valley, like David did, we need someone to be the 'consciousness of God'. At those times God's presence can seem so distant, uninvolved and detached. We find ourselves asking, 'Where is God in all this?' Joining someone in their valley enables God to use us as His reassuring presence that they're not alone by themselves.

'I'll be back soon', a World War II soldier told his wife before leaving her and their infant son. Five years of war and fighting went by. The young mother would show her boy a portrait of the soldier and say, 'See, that's your daddy. One day he's coming home.' In reality, she didn't know what to expect. One morning the boy said, 'Mummy, wouldn't it be great if Daddy would just step out of the picture frame and come home?'

Sometimes people need God to step out of the bigger picture into their valley of trouble. You and I can be that person, the conscious and tangible presence of God on their journey. Vera Nazarian said, 'Sometimes, reaching out and taking someone's hand is the beginning of a journey.'[4]

## The resource of your journey

Our lives consist of journey past, those things we've been through; journey present, things we're currently processing; and journey future, things that are yet be. God comes alongside us on our journey, with its own particular and unique experiences, giving us something for someone else on theirs. He deposits in us things to share with them.

Our journey experience, our 'valley', our 'struggle', our 'hard time', has significance for someone else. In the Church in recent years there's been a lot of teaching on gifts: gifts of the Spirit, personal gifts, spiritual gifts, natural gifts, temperaments, personality traits, etc. But there's a largely neglected gift. A gift we bring to church each week, sit with in church, then take home with us and do nothing with it. Then we bring it back again to church the following week.

I describe this gift as our 'resource of journey'. There are people in our churches, who have experienced deep struggles of the soul and difficult circumstances; who've been through business issues, parental issues, family issues, divorce issues, rejection issues, debt issues, bereavement issues, and many other struggles. Some of these may have been your own experience. This is the great resource of our journey. However, this resource remains a largely untapped reservoir of vast life experience; a rich, unmined vein of resource God wants to use. If we can recognise and take this resource God has deposited in us, and understand how to bring it alongside someone else struggling with similar circumstances, suddenly it becomes a gift God has given us, to give to others. We can take something significant we have, making it available to someone else.

God doesn't comfort us to make us comfortable; He comforts us to make us comforters. God has placed resources in every Christian that when released from one person and received by another can bring about healing and change. I am convinced that this is the healing community God calls us to be. 'I am continuously thanking my God for you when I think about the grace God has offered you in Jesus the Anointed. *In this grace,* God is enriching every aspect of your lives by gifting you with the right words to say and everything you need to know. In this way, your life story confirms the life story of the Anointed One, so you are not ill-equipped or slighted on any necessary gifts' (1 Cor. 1:4–7, TV).

Our journey has been moulding us, not only bringing shape, quality and purpose to our life, but also for a greater good. What has happened on our journey is exactly what it has needed to be. At the time it was hard, confusing and painful. It left us shattered and devastated. But the road of recovery has been our experience. The sustaining grace of God has brought us through. His truth has brought insight, perspective, guidance and direction. Others have given strength and support. Our spiritual journey, beginning when we encountered the love and forgiveness of Jesus at the cross, has enabled us to embrace that love and live freely in it.

You may think you've lost time or wasted years because of what you've been through, but there are no shortcuts in life. In God's purposes nothing is lost or wasted. It has taken each and every situation you've encountered to bring you to where you are now. And now is the right time to make your 'resource of journey' available to others. Journey is a God-given process in which we grow and change in response to circumstances as God helps us overcome and find victory, and this can be true of your experiences.

## Give your gift away

I beg you, don't hide this precious, hard fought-for gift. Don't keep it under wraps, buried in the pews of your church. This rich vein of spiritual resource is made available through Jesus Christ in the family of God, a wealth of life experience and spiritual vitality deposited in the lives of God's people must not be wasted. If you're part of a church of 100 people with an average age of 50, then there's 5,000 years of journey experience sitting in your pews each week. If we allowed God to release that into needs amongst the congregation, and beyond the walls of the church into the community, what an impact we would make.

Paul writes, 'I feel certain that you, my brothers, have real Christian character and experience, and that you are capable of keeping each other on the right road' (Rom. 15:14, JB Phillips). When God gives us gifts, they're for giving away, to be shared with others. If you're not sharing your gift – your resource of journey – with others, then start journeying with someone and share your gift today!

A century from now it's unlikely that anyone will recall your name, where you lived, what you did or what you had, but the world will have been a different and better place this century because you were willing to journey with someone else, to share the richness of your resource of journey with the needy of this world.

I read an account of Chuck Colson in an article that said, 'He often asked himself why he had to go to prison as a result of Watergate. Legally, there was no reason why he should have been put in prison. Nevertheless, he ended up there, and, for a long time, he struggled with that. Why did he have to suffer the humiliation, the shame, the disgrace, and the discontent of prison? But then the answer began to come. While he was in prison he learned what prisoners go through. He saw these forgotten men and women of American society, the awful injustices they often face, the difficulty, even the impossibility of recovering themselves, and there was born in him a great sense of compassion and a desire to help. After he was released from prison, he devoted his whole life and ministry to going back in and helping these men. Now wonderful stories are coming out from prisons all over America of dramatic changes in human lives because Chuck Colson was sent to prison.'[5] Chuck Colson used his resource of journey, and the impact of grace and truth in his life, to change the lives of others. As the saying goes, 'a lot of people have gone further than they thought they could, because someone else thought they could.'

## Fellow travellers

You may think your life experience is ordinary, of no consequence. That your story has no relevance to other people's lives, that you don't have what it takes, but that couldn't be further from the truth. You say, 'but I feel inadequate for the task. I am not a counsellor, psychotherapist, or experienced social worker; they may need expert help.' Well, in some cases that may be true, but in my experience of church life, in the vast majority of situations it's not. People who are struggling need fellow travellers with a resource of journey who can walk well with them. Just walking alongside, entering into their lives, listening, talking, laughing, crying, praying. Someone said, 'A good companion on a journey makes the way seem shorter.'

You might say, 'But I'm struggling with something myself; how could I be of help?' Dr Karl Menninger once gave a lecture on mental health and answered questions from the audience. Someone asked, 'What would you advise a person to do if that person felt a nervous breakdown coming on?' Most people thought he'd say, 'Go see a psychiatrist immediately,' but he didn't. To their astonishment. Dr Menninger replied, 'Lock up your house, go across the railroad tracks, find somebody in need, and help that person. Don't focus on yourself. Get involved in the lives of other people.'[6]

Remember our text: 'He comes alongside us when we go through hard times, and before you know it, He brings us alongside someone else who is going through hard times, so that we can be there for that person just as God was there for us' (2 Cor. 1:3, MSG). These verses are clearly inclusive not exclusive, written to the Church, the body of Christ, not the professionals. It doesn't matter where we are along our journey, we can walk a few steps with someone else. It's a matter of putting one foot in front of the other.

## You've got what it takes

We don't need to have the exact same experience as others. If God has in any way been our help in a hard place we can know with confidence He'll provide that same help in someone else's time of trouble also, maybe through us. Your story may not be the same but your experience of grace and truth in a time of struggle is just as relevant to their struggle. As you've received God's mercy, comfort and strength, so He'll enable you to share and impart that to others as you walk with them. It's your experience of God's grace in hard times that qualifies you to journey with others in their hard times.

Joining someone on their journey says, 'I'm here and I care'. Believe me that it's so desperately needed by so many. Often we think that to help we've got to do something. We feel an unspoken pressure to make something positive happen. The fact of the matter is we don't need to 'do' something, we need to 'be' something.

There's an old adage with some truth in it that Jesus taught the 'be-atitudes', not the 'do-atitudes'. Our reassuring presence on the journey is our 'being' there. Coming alongside someone doesn't mean we're responsible for rescuing them. Resist the urge to fix people or to jump in to rescue them. Learn to walk alongside them as they trust God, and journey with them, providing resources of support. When we have experienced His presence for ourselves through others, it is with gratitude and thankfulness we can willingly make ourselves available.

Have you heard of Jean Nidetch? Her struggle was that she was a 214-pound homemaker desperate to lose weight. She went to the New York City Department of Health, where she was given a diet devised by Dr Norman Jolliffe. Two months later, discouraged about the 50-plus pounds still to go, she invited six overweight friends home to share the diet and talk about how to stay on it. And so, in 1963, their journey together with their significant life issue began. Today, more than one million members attend about 29,000 Weight Watchers meetings in 30 countries every week.

Why was Nidetch able to help people take control of their lives? To answer that, she tells a story. When she was a teenager, she used to cross a park where she saw mothers gossiping while the toddlers sat on their swings, with no one to push them. 'I'd give them a push', says Nidetch. 'And you know what happens when you push a kid on a swing? Pretty soon he's pumping, doing it himself. That's what my role in life is – I'm there to give others a push.'[7]

## Commonality of the journey

When we begin to share with each other what our journeys have been, often there are incredible similarities. The underlying dynamics of life are pretty much the same for all of us. Joys and sadnesses, successes and failures, happiness and disappointments, acceptance and rejection, order and confusion, stress and calm, gains and losses, love and fear, hurt and healing, pain and comfort, and so on. These are the highs and lows we all go through at different points on our journey. When we're willing to open up our stories and life journeys to each other we often find in a congregation a commonality of life experience. This becomes an incredible opening to engage together in opportunities both inside and outside the church. In fact, our talents are best used when we combine them with the talents of others. There is something about doing things together that makes the sum of the whole greater than its individual parts. The professionals call this synergy. The Holy Spirit is the master of synergy.

When we received the call to pastor in New Zealand I was excited by the opportunity and accepted the position. Deb hadn't anticipated such a major life change and move to the other side of the world to unknown surroundings and a new culture. As is often the case when you arrive at a new church, everyone is extremely welcoming and friendly. But in a sense it can be a bit like a bereavement in that after six months, everyone goes back to their normal patterns of life and leaves you to get on with yours. After the initial period, Deb struggled to adjust in a new big city, a new country, a new church, a new home, far away from friends and family and all that was familiar. She felt somewhat disoriented, and unsettled.

After some months, she got to know several other ladies who had similarly come to New Zealand with their husbands; another lady from the UK, one from America, another from Singapore. They journeyed together with their shared experience of coming to a new city and country. After a while, they realised there must be hundreds of other women coming to the city whom they could reach out to and journey with, even with simple things like finding schools, hairdressers, shopping and the like. They printed cards under the heading 'Moving On After Moving In' (MOAMI) and posted them on notice boards around the city, in libraries, food store pin boards, and community notice boards, inviting women new to the city to contact them for an orientation session. Soon they were receiving calls. They arranged sessions for them in one of the church rooms then took them round the city, showing them schools, shops and things they needed to know, coming alongside them over weeks and months. Some of the women started coming to church. This is the journey resource at work, synergised and energised by the Holy Spirit.

## CHAPTER 6

# Lion and bear stories

'Let *the good news*, the story you have heard from the beginning of your journey, live in *and take hold of you*' (1 John 2:24, TV)

Today and every day our life journey continues. 'It is good to have an end to journey toward, but it is the journey that matters in the end.'[1] The journey, intrinsic to our story, is only part of the picture of who and what we are. We're children of God, with insights of grace and truth that have shaped and moulded us as we've travelled life's highway. And that's who we've become today. Not simply the sum of our life experiences, a compilation of facts or a catalogue of interesting statistics, but a product of what those experiences have taught and made us, and more significantly, what the power of Christ has wrought in us on the anvil of life. We are new creations in Christ being transformed daily into His image. Our lives through the power of Christ have been a process of transformation; His life, impacting our journey.

## The significance of your journey

Each of us who have come to Christ have a story to share of grace, mercy, truth, forgiveness, and the goodness of God; the intervention of God's dealings and working on our journey, no matter how joyful, painful, sad, tragic, confusing or difficult it may have been. It's an individual story of what He's done in our lives. We are formed not simply by experiences and struggles we've encountered, happy or traumatic events we may have gone through, but rather by how we've dealt with and managed them in the light of grace and truth. And this is what the resource of journey is all about, reaching out to others with our experience of God's grace and compassion. The very life issues we've faced are ones others are struggling with. Yet so often we fail to allow God to use those experiences to reach out and touch their lives.

Over the years I've built up what I call my 'lion and bear' stories. I have a file that contains them that I continually add to. They are milestones and markers, and I've included a few in this book. Remember the Old Testament story when the Israelites had come to the point of facing defeat and extinction at the hands of the Philistines. David stood before Saul, offering his help, and Saul turned him down. David said, 'But King Saul, you don't know about my lion and bear stories, when God's power enabled me to triumph in adversity.' Then he proceeded to tell how with God's enabling he'd slain and killed a lion and bear in God's strength. And, as they say, the rest of the story is history, spoken of even to this day. The outcome all hinged on his 'lion and bear' stories. Whether you realise it or not, you have your own 'lion and bear' stories to tell.

And just in case you thought your journey was irrelevant, that your story was of no consequence, well ... surprise! It's of great consequence! It has consequence for the lives of others, impacting and helping them on their journey. In the big picture of this battle, David seemed insignificant, but it turned out that his 'lion and bear' stories had huge consequences for the nation of Israel. Like David, your journey counts too!

There's nothing more motivating when you're struggling than hearing from someone who's been able to overcome similar struggles. I recall not long after my kidney cancer diagnosis and surgery receiving a call from a neighbour I barely knew who'd also just been diagnosed with kidney cancer. Then, a little while later, someone else who also faced the same difficult challenge and just recently a member of my own family. My journey had relevance to their journey and I had the joy and privilege to travel alongside them.

If we're willing, God can use us to reach out to others struggling with similar life issues we've already processed. People have been restored, healed, strengthened and converted when they've listened to someone who has trodden that pathway before them, and cared enough to reach out. An old saying goes: 'An ounce of experience is worth a ton of theory.' How true. I can almost guarantee the person who influenced you most in your Christian life was themselves someone who had experienced the grace of God in their own life struggles. When we hear how God has worked in the life of another it raises hope and faith in us, giving us strength. Someone has said, 'Your life is a journey, not a destination.'

## Understanding our journey narrative

One of the most powerful ways of impacting people is through the compelling power of storytelling. The Cambridge dictionary defines 'narrative' as the 'description of a series of events: a particular way of explaining or understanding events'.[2] To be effective with our personal narratives it's important to review, clarify and fully understand our past journey, and to be able to articulate and connect to someone struggling with similar issues.

Some think we shouldn't look backwards or inwards, they tell us it's unhealthy, introspective, narcissistic, even self-indulgent; that as new creations in Christ we should look forward and embrace our future in Him. They draw attention to Paul's words in Philippians 3:13–14, 'forgetting those things which are behind and reaching forward to those things which are ahead, I press toward the goal for the prize of the upward call of God in Christ Jesus'. However, what seems to be missed is the fact that Paul recounted the story of his journey to the Corinthians (2 Cor. 11–12). He tells in some detail of his severe suffering and struggles. He didn't divorce his journey past from his journey present or future. In reality, personal history and current narrative cannot be separated.

It's good to look forward, '"For I know the plans that I have for you," declares the LORD, "plans for welfare and not for calamity to give you a future and a hope"' (Jer. 29:11, NASB), but if we separate the present from the past we live in denial. I take no issue with an emphasis on embracing the future but that doesn't mean a disassociation from the past. Forgetting the past doesn't mean denying the past. Faith isn't the denial of reality but trusting God in the face of reality. That's what our 'lion and bear' stories are all about. It is the healthy person who is able to consider and look back at their journey. On numerous occasions in Scripture God exhorts us to remember … remember … remember …

## Looking backwards, moving forwards

It doesn't make sense to ignore our own past; to not consider or learn from our history. We gain insight and understanding from our successes and failures, our triumphs and tragedies, achievements and mistakes. The Chinese sage and philosopher Confucius says, 'Study the past if you would define the future'. If we refuse to look back we'll never have a story to tell or journey to recount. The important thing to take into the future is what we've gained from the process of the past. This is what testimony is all about: recounting the goodness of God in our history, on our journey. The perspective of a fellow traveller can help us travel well even though the pathway may be bumpy and uncomfortable. The reality of their life lessons and insights can become part of the understanding of our own journey.

What is unhealthy is to live in the past, preoccupied with shadows and ghosts that haunt and taunt us, continually glancing over our shoulder, allowing unresolved past conflicts to reverberate, negatively impacting our lives today. If we're going to look back, we need to look all the way back to the cross, viewing our journey from the perspective of Calvary.

The message of the gospel is that grace and forgiveness have cancelled out the ongoing impact and power of past sins and failure. 'He has forgiven you all your sins: Christ has utterly wiped out the damning evidence of broken laws and commandments which always hung over our heads, and has completely annulled it by nailing it over his own head on the cross. And then, having drawn the sting of all the powers ranged against us, he exposed them, shattered, empty and defeated, in his final glorious triumphant act!' (Col. 2:14, Phillips).

If we don't allow grace, truth and forgiveness to 'draw the sting' at the cross, writing off the negative effects of the past, neutralising and annulling them, they'll rob us of positive possibilities of our future. We all have a past; take it to the cross, receive grace, truth and forgiveness, then, with the help of God and those around us, proceed to live full, meaningful lives despite the sometimes lasting physical or psychological effects of our past. This is what Paul is talking about when he says, 'forgetting those things which are behind and reaching forward to those things which are ahead, I press toward the goal for the prize of the upward call of God in Christ Jesus' (Phil. 3:13–14).

Looking both backwards and forwards is best understood by a rower on a lake, who balances going forward while looking backward. The rower rows towards a distant point on the shore and as he rows forward, he looks back at the place he's come from. Gazing back on his journey completed so far, he rows forward in the passage he's now on. There is a clear symmetry here between moving forward while looking backwards. As the rower looks back to the distant shore, the further he gets away from his start point the greater his perspective, the wider his vista, the grander his view, the larger his horizon, the bigger the picture giving him his bearings. What he looks back at becomes his reference point going forward. You see, as we move forwards, our perspective on the past enables us to see with greater understanding the goodness of God going forward.

This may seem counter intuitive as most people look forward to go forward, but if we don't recognise all we've learned from our past, there may not be much to our future, because God uses our past as part of His future. It has shaped what we bring to our future and plays a part in where we are going. Our successes and failures, triumphs and tragedies, achievements and mistakes are the things God uses in the lives of others.

## Map or itinerary?

I am sure many of us might like to be able to rewrite parts of our life story. We may all have pages or chapters we'd like to go back and edit, even rip out and throw on an open fire. 'Ah', you lament to yourself, 'if only I'd had a map or, even better, a sat nav with its dulcet tones giving me clear and specific directions, my journey may have taken a different turn.' These days life mapping has almost become a science, but I question whether or not there can be such a thing. I guess my response is both yes and no. Let me explain.

A map is a predetermined set of fixed parameters that are certain and established; however, as we look forward to the future, even though we may plan, is it possible to have such a map for life? *If only*, we wish. This is how Robert Burns put it in his famous poem *To A Mouse*:

'But, Mousie, thou art no thy lane [you aren't alone] In proving foresight may be vain: The best laid schemes o' mice an' men Gang aft a-gley, [often go awry] An'lea'e us [and leave us] nought but grief an' pain, For promis'd joy!'[3]

I've even heard people say the Bible is God's road map, but going forward in life there are no certainties, no fixed parameters, no road map for life. We can never know the detail of what the future holds – it is not predictable. Life happens.

However, it is possible to set out an itinerary. Ah, that's different. An itinerary points the way ahead, sets a direction for moving forward. The dictionary describes it as a list of places to visit or to stop at. A series of landmarks, milestones, markers and signposts along the way. There could be many different ways, or a whole number of varied routes to get to an eventual destination. An itinerary basically sketches an outline of a potential route. Coming from the Latin word *itiner*, which means 'to journey'.

The Bible isn't simply a road map or even an itinerary – it's a story, and a romantic story at that. But that story reveals milestones, landmarks, markers, and signposts for our journey. This is what the life of Christ is all about. The biggest milestone and marker in God's story is the cross of Christ. All Old Testament truths converge on it, all New Testament truths emerge out of it. It is the signpost back to God. It is the pivotal point of His story, His journey. It changes everything.

## Follow me, lad!

Your story is an itinerary of milestones, landmarks, markers and signposts; a guide for someone else's journey. In that sense your journey can become their itinerary, their guide.

I remember going to the city of Belfast many years ago without a map and getting lost. I approached a policeman to see if he could help me to get where I wanted to go. 'Have you a map, lad?' he asked, 'No', I replied. 'Right then', he said, 'follow me, lad, I am your map; I will get you to where you want to go.' And with that he marched off, with me in tow. We journeyed together for about twenty minutes across the city, with him pointing out landmarks and markers along the way, even a better and shorter route. 'Way better than the tourist map', he assured me. Then he pointed me to a sign post. 'Follow that from here on, lad' he said, 'and you won't go wrong.' He knew the way, he'd trodden it before many times, and I duly arrived safely at my destination.

Isn't that what Jesus said to the disciples, 'I am the way ... follow me', then He set off on a three-year journey with them that led them to the cross. He was their itinerary. Journeying is at the heart of discipleship. No wonder the Early Church described themselves as the people of 'the Way'. Paul could say, 'Follow me as I follow Christ' (1 Cor. 11:1, MEV), and to the Colossians, 'but which is now as clear as daylight to those who love God. They are those to whom God has planned to give a vision of the full wonder and splendour of his secret plan for the sons of men. And the secret is simply this: Christ in you! Yes, Christ in you bringing with him the hope of all glorious things to come' (Col. 1:26–27, Phillips).

## The power of your story

We live in a culture where stories are so important. People relate to stories better than anything – they have undeniable power. Books, newspapers, movies and TV are all built upon stories; they're the basis of these multi-billion pound industries, and the Bible is the most epic story of all time. It's a divine casebook with true-to-life accounts of people touched by God.

We all love a good story. How well I remember being a small child on Sunday evenings in the winter, huddled around our small fireplace. Dad would stoke it high with coal until the flames roared up the chimney. He'd turn the lights out and the special treat would begin. A slice of toast on the toasting fork held near the flames and then he would start. Long, long ago, in a land far away … and for the next hour he would enthrall and regale us with a magical story.

Never underestimate the power of storytelling, especially stories about what God is doing with your life. Stories challenge, inspire, inform, encourage, guide and strengthen. Telling your personal story is the best way to help someone gain a clearer picture of their circumstances. A story hooks into our feelings, emotions, minds, and imaginations. This is why Jesus used everyday stories – parables – to communicate the nature of the kingdom of God.

God has spoken in story and we'd do well to listen to the way He has told it. We can never fully understand or make sense of our story until we see it as part of a bigger story, God's greater story. 'Keep your eyes on *Jesus*, who both began and finished this race we're in. Study how he did it … When you find yourselves flagging in your faith, go over that story again, item by item, that long litany of hostility he plowed through. *That* will shoot adrenaline into your souls!' (Heb. 12:2–3, MSG).

## Crystallise your journey

Your story is unique and worth listening to. No, it isn't complete or perfect, it continues with new pages every day and fresh chapters every week. Maybe you've never had chance to write your personal story and journey down. Let me encourage you to think about it. If you can take time just to sketch an outline of it, then you'll begin to have a clear idea of what your story is about, not because you don't know your story, but because it will crystallise key areas that may be helpful to others and connect points to their journey. Taking time to consider and scan our own story brings an awareness of its potential, and a recognition of the resources God has deposited in our lives. The more clearly we understand this, the better equipped we are to effectively come alongside others.

We all have key spiritual transitions in our lives that we can plot; things we can identify in our 'lion and bear' file. Think back and clarify the significant milestones and markers on your journey that have had the most impact on you. They might fall into one of these categories:

- Unforeseen circumstances such as a child or partner suffering a disability, redundancy, death, sickness, financial setbacks.
- Personal struggles such as failure, disappointment, identity, rejection, vocation.
- Relationships such as marriage, family, singlehood, relational style, early childhood impact.

Every journey narrative contains ingredients and components that go into making up our story – contributing elements and factors that have played an important part in the circumstances and events. These are the feelings and emotions underlying our struggles; the actions, reactions and responses we've experienced. Negative thought patterns or self-talk that maybe were part of the cause or consequence of what happened. How we've been able to face and process challenges and concerns. Identifying major influences shaping attitudes and choices. Coping with common life experiences and daily demands in life. How we've been able to handle and process them enables us to come alongside others to care for and help them with insights and perspective gained, personal growth and development experienced, and outcomes that have been meaningful and significant.

## Go tell your story

At the heart of the story is our spiritual journey, our walk with the Lord, even though at times it has faltered, and we haven't always got it right. But we have made progress on our journey of grace and truth, and even when stumbling and struggling we've gained spiritual insight and direction. We've come to understand spiritual values and beliefs that have sustained us, giving perspective, strength, hope and optimism. Even when we've failed, we've found forgiveness and restoration, gaining knowledge and wisdom from understanding our own weaknesses and strengths. We're not perfect, but God continues His ongoing transforming work in our lives, like a potter with the clay.

Maybe you say to yourself, 'But my story is kind of personal. I'm not sure I want to share it with others.' Well, always remember we can share a lot of ourselves without revealing all of the detailed facts about ourselves. Think of your story as having chapters. Open up the chapter you're comfortable with and share that. God will use it. If you're still feeling vulnerable with other chapters, then allow God to bring someone alongside to help you explore that chapter. Always remember that your story is one of redemption, reconciliation and restoration – track it all the way back to the cross, and let Him meet you there. Always remember, every great journey starts with a few small steps.

The purpose of telling your story is to enable you to journey better with others; to bring as sharply into focus as possible the reality of your life and relationship with God that has enabled you to process it well. There is a saying that expression deepens impression, that's to say that often it's not until we begin to share something in detail with one another that events and situations fall into an even greater perspective and understanding for us. So, go tell your story.

## CHAPTER 7

# Journeying – Jesus style

'We have plenty of hard times that come from following the Messiah, but no more so than the good times of his healing comfort [*paraclesis*] — we get a full measure of that, too.' (2 Cor. 1:5, MSG)

The setting is two dejected, disillusioned, downcast disciples returning home after their dreams of a new dawn are left shattered by the death of their leader. They're wrestling with their broken dreams and dashed hopes, consumed by sadness and overwhelmed by grief. They're walking away from a grave, a rich man's tomb. It is where their highest hopes have just been left, dead and buried with this man Jesus. Now it is the end, and the long walk home to Emmaus has begun. Rather than the new world order they're expecting, they're heading back to a broken world of the same old, same old. They're deeply disconsolate and if any men ever needed consolation [*paraclesis*] and encouragement [*parakaleo*], they did. Disconsolation is the expression of loss, grief, sorrow, disappointment, failure, and hopelessness. That's exactly where they were: forlorn, heart broken, grief stricken, bereaved, and distressed. Let's pick up the story in Luke 24, closing in with Jesus as He joins their journey. Let's observe the Divine *Paraclete*, the Divine Consoler, at work.

## Joining the journey

The journey from Jerusalem to Emmaus is not a ten yards dash, or a casual country stroll. The town of Emmaus was around seven miles from Jerusalem over a fairly rugged road, maybe 3–4 hours' walk away. When Jesus approaches them He understands He's in for the long haul. This was a serious walk to undertake and He'll walk beside them every step of the way. As He encounters these disciples He gives us a model or pattern for journeying – Jesus style.

The passage says, 'two of them were travelling that same day to a village called Emmaus, which was *about* seven miles from Jerusalem' (Luke 24:13). Notice it says here, 'that same day'. What day is that? It is resurrection day and this is late afternoon. Jesus, now raised to new life, having already appeared to Mary in the garden, appears to these two dejected and forlorn guys walking back down the road of disillusionment and abandonment.

It's a hugely significant account. Jesus, just risen from the dead, and who will after 40 days ascend to His Father, intentionally chooses to seek out two hurting men struggling to cope. It is compelling to realise that the very first thing Jesus does in the post-resurrection era is come alongside and journey with men in their valley of trouble. Here, back doing ministry, the first ministry engagement of Jesus, the risen Lord, is to journey with troubled people. This is the first role He assumes in the new order of things. Don't you think Jesus is making a huge statement here, and laying down a clear marker that journeying has a significant place and role in our lives?

This journey took place even before He'd appeared to His other frightened disciples, who were penned up like sheep, fearing for their lives and future. It was only when the two disciples on the road to Emmaus got back to Jerusalem following their encounter with Jesus, that the Scripture says, 'they told about the things *that had happened* on the road, and how He was known to them in the breaking of bread.Now as they said these things, Jesus Himself stood in the midst of them, and said to them, "Peace to you"' (Luke 24:35–36). 'And He led them out as far as Bethany, and He lifted up His hands and blessed them. Now it came to pass, while He blessed them, that He was parted from them and carried up into heaven' (vv50–51). No question then, this journey is of great importance.

## Everyone has a story to tell

They were deep in conversation, reliving, retelling the shocking events of the past week: 'They were talking with each other about everything that had happened' (v14, NIV). They had so many unanswered questions as they tried to make sense of the tragedy. Their lives had been turned upside down. In their minds they played over and over again what could have been, might have been, should have been. They'd hoped for a last minute miracle, but now their hopes for the future were dashed and gone. For them their present reality was part of a living memory.

There is a backstory here – there always is a backstory. They'd been longing, hoping for years – centuries – for their Messiah, and for three years had become convinced this man Jesus was the Saviour and Deliverer of Israel. This was their dream, their hope. Now the memory of the centuries is linked to their current experience.

They had had just seen that hope and dream dissolve and evaporate. Not a three-year personal dream, but the dream of the centuries of a nation. Now they are speaking the language of despair, trying to make sense of the enormity of it. They're in confusion, and when we're in confusion we play things over and over again in our minds. Psychologists call this the inner monologue, or self-talk, so when something happens, a present reality is linked to a past memory compounding it. This connects the painful memories of the backstory to the present difficult living reality, distorting current cognition with a whole raft of emotions and reactions. Journeying allows someone to begin to express the inner monologue, confusion, turmoil and pain.

## Connecting with their story

'As they talked and discussed these things with each other, Jesus himself came up and walked along with them' (Luke 24:15, NIV). Jesus doesn't just come and stand close or put a hand on their shoulder; He becomes part of their journey, walking beside them. He approaches, slips up from behind, catches up and falls in step. He doesn't ambush them but gets alongside them in the moment. Notice that He doesn't gatecrash or attempt to take over the conversation.

Some people don't want to listen when they join a conversation, they want to talk. A self-centred person just barges in, hijacks, dominates, and controls the conversation. They immediately want to tell you all about themselves. They are like opera stars warming up for the big performance, 'Me, me, me, me, me!' Journeying starts by just showing up and 'being there', not wanting to talk about ourselves but providing a listening ear. Our presence on someone's journey is fifty per cent of the care that God wants us to bring. One of the old gospel songs puts it, 'and He walks with me and He talks with me and He tells me that I am His own'.[1]

Patiently He walks beside them. Deep in conversation, they don't recognise Him, 'but they were kept from recognising him' (v16, NIV). The last thing they were expecting was His company as a fellow traveller. He is not intrusive. He doesn't impose Himself or His views on them. He doesn't startle or shock them with the revelation of who He is or what He is about. He could have done that by declaring, 'I'm risen from the dead. It's me, Jesus.' He doesn't do that. Instead, He takes time to build rapport. His quiet, calm, reassuring, peaceful presence: the consoler. Consolation is the first step of journeying, bringing and being the peace of God, the calm of Christ.

## Listening to their story

He makes a gentle enquiry, 'What kind of conversation *is* this that you have with one another as you walk and are sad?' (v17). He is saying, 'Help me understand what you're talking about', an open-ended question to draw them out. Their response is indignant: 'Are you the only stranger in Jerusalem, and have you not known the things which happened there in these days?' (v18).

The trial had been the top news story and they seem incredulous He would not have been aware. But He's gently drawing attention to the pain of their sadness: 'And he said to them, "What things?"' (v19). Do you think He asks because He doesn't know what has happened? Why, He had been at the centre of the story, the main subject and focus of all the recent events. He knows exactly what's happened, but wants to give them the opportunity to talk out their experiences of those events. So He uses this door opener, 'What things?' so that they can tell their story and express their deepest feelings.

Notice He said to them, 'as you walk and are sad'. He's listening to their conversation, He has said nothing, but He's hearing something deeper than the words He's listening to. He identifies their painful feeling and reflects it to them. Using these words He expresses His empathy, 'I sense you are feeling sad'. He is not invasive, He didn't say, 'you guys are obviously upset, now what's this all about?' He reads their body language, looking at their faces, the way they're walking, the way their shoulders were slumped. He was reading the signals they're sending out. When we come alongside we need to be careful to be warm, genuine, attentive, tender and authentic. He allows them time to express their emotions. He is inviting them to 'tell me about it'. He hasn't said anything yet other than use a conversation opener to help them to express more. Believe it or not, most people don't want your sympathy or even advice – they just want to be heard and understood.

## Let them tell their story

"'About Jesus of Nazareth," they replied. "He was a prophet, powerful in word and deed before God and all the people. The chief priests and our rulers handed him over to be sentenced to death, and they crucified him; but we had hoped that he was the one who was going to redeem Israel'" (Luke 24:19–21, NIV). He keeps walking and listening, letting them tell their story in their own way and time. He didn't hurry them up. How long does He walk? As long as it takes, He's in for the long haul. It's all so fresh to them so He just lets them keep talking. He's listening attentively, not thinking about what He is going to say next.

He allows them to unburden their hearts: 'And what is more, it is the third day since all this took place. In addition, some of our women amazed us. They went to the tomb early this morning but didn't find his body. They came and told us that they had seen a vision of angels, who said he was alive. Then some of our companions went to the tomb and found it just as the women had said, but they did not see Jesus' (vv21–24, NIV).

They're probably halfway through the journey by now. When you journey with someone it takes time to let them tell their story and unburden their heart. They want this stranger to know and understand their broken world. He doesn't cut them short, but continues to listen to their story. He had the answer – rather, He *is* the answer – but He wanted them to discover it. He could have imposed it on them as soon as He met them, but He understands the importance of the process of journey. Having built rapport, shown understanding, demonstrated empathy and committed Himself to their journey, He now starts to bring hope and perspective to their world.

## Care-fronting

What does that mean? Well it certainly doesn't mean confronting or rebuking. He walks with them, listens intently to them. He has demonstrated He cares and now He talks with them. Care-fronting is showing care and concern for the individual, affirming them, not just challenging, rationalising or focusing on the issue. It is not so much trying to change the person or even change their circumstances, but trying to help them see themselves and their circumstances more accurately, bringing perspective and hope; truth in the context of grace. It involves three things:

1. Having taken time to understand, feel their pain and show respect, Jesus has earned the right to speak. They are now willing to listen to what He has to say. We cannot speak effectively unless we know and understand how people feel, because when people feel understood, they will listen to what we have to say.

2. He helps them face reality. 'How foolish you are' (v25, NIV). That doesn't mean, 'you stupid idiots'. The Greek word for foolish here means a lack of understanding. They were failing to understand something here. J.B. Phillips puts it, 'Aren't you failing to understand, and slow to believe'. The Amplified version puts it, 'O, foolish men, and slow of heart to trust'. He wants them to understand the reality of their own perception of the circumstances.

3. The same verse in the Amplified version continues, '*and* believe in everything that the prophets have spoken!' (v25). He then focuses them on perspective and hope: the prophets. They were struggling with a two-fold problem here, a head problem (the loss of perspective), and a heart problem (a lack of belief and loss of hope). Hope directly relates to perspective. Knowing they are familiar with the prophets, He takes their inner monologue, their subjective reality, and relates it to objective truth. He goes head to head with doubt and unbelief by exposing it to truth. If we've walked with God and He's brought grace and truth to us in our struggle then we have found grace, truth, perspective and hope. This is at the heart of care-fronting.

## Telling His story

Now He begins to unfold some perspective: "'Did not the Messiah have to suffer these things and then enter his glory?" And beginning with

Moses and all the Prophets, he explained to them what was said in all the Scriptures concerning himself' (vv26–27, NIV). This is not an Old Testament history lesson or a Bible study. 'And beginning with Moses and all the Prophets, he explained'. He talks to them about objective truth they were familiar with: the Messiah. He then talks about His own reality: things concerning Himself, His circumstances, His suffering, His life, His story, His journey. Even His pain and confusion that caused Him to call out in the words of Psalm 22:1, 'My God, my God, why have you forsaken me?' He journeys on with them, linking His story to their story, to God's story.

He brings to them both grace and truth. He's been gracious in His walking with them, listening to them for a big part of the journey. Now, letting grace flow towards them, it's time for truth. It is said of Jesus, by John, 'we beheld his glory ... full of grace and truth' (John 1:14). When grace precedes truth, the glory of Christ is to be seen. Truth is not harsh and cold and detached, but full of vitality and life-giving in the context of grace. Jesus said on one occasion, 'The words that I speak to you are spirit, and *they* are life' (John 6:63). When we take the time to let grace flow, walking and journeying, then living truth will flow on from there. That's what our *paraclesis* verses say: 2 Corinthians 1:4 says that He comes alongside us, so that as we come alongside others and we can be there for that person, allowing the grace and truth in us to flow through us. Grace and truth bring perspective and hope, and hope is at the heart of journeying.

## Enlightenment dawns

By His listening and sharing He ministers to their need: 'As they approached the village to which they were going, Jesus continued on as if he were going further. But they urged him strongly, "Stay with us, for it is nearly evening; the day is almost over." So he went in to stay with them. When he was at the table with them, he took bread, gave thanks, broke it and began to give it to them' (Luke 24:28–30, NIV). He was listening and sharing so much that when they get to their village they almost forgot where they live. So engrossed are they in the stories being exchanged, they don't want it to stop here, they want it to continue. This is seven miles on, a journey of about four hours. Something is happening here. As they've journeyed, the risen Lord Jesus has been imparting grace and truth to them. It is as though Jesus says to them, 'I've got to journey on', but they say, 'No, this is so meaningful to us, something has been happening to us on the journey, come in and be with us – stay with us'. They invite Him in and He goes in at their bidding. In journeying, He has become a caring friend, a trusted confidante, and a travelling companion, gaining their confidence and trust. The risen Christ of grace and truth has been pouring Himself into their lives. Now they are so connected with this stranger that they want Him to stay with them. Now they're not walking, they are sitting, resting in His presence, communing, sharing grace and truth.

In this process of imparting grace and truth, enlightenment dawns into their darkened world: 'Then their eyes were opened and they recognised him' (v31, NIV). He takes bread, breaks it as they have a meal, somehow a light is turned on in their souls, 'and he disappeared from their sight'. Suddenly He's gone, the hard place has been navigated, the valley has been crossed, the journey travelled, the mission accomplished. Realisation dawns in their spirit, scales fall from eyes as He slips out of sight and vanishes from view. This is the moment of epiphany, their eyes are opened. An *Ah-ha!* moment, a light bulb moment. Light dawns as His presence is made known them. They look at each other; it was Him, just what they needed in their hour of struggle. Paul prays for the Ephesians that, 'the eyes of your understanding being enlightened; that you may know what is the hope of His calling, what are the riches of the glory of His inheritance in the saints' (Eph. 1:18).

Turning to each other, they ask, 'Were not our hearts burning within us while he talked with us on the road and opened the Scriptures to us?' (Luke 24:32, NIV). It was almost as though one disciple said, 'I was seeing something, but I was feeling something too; my feelings of disconsolation and dejection started to change somehow. In fact, it felt like my heart was catching fire. How about you?' And as if the other responded back,

'Yes, I was feeling my heart burning, too. My heart was changing as my mind was comprehending what Jesus was opening to us of His story'. They didn't compare notes, they compared hearts. They had received a visitation of divine light and divine heat. As enlightenment dawns in their spirit they suddenly realise that there are other people to journey with, too, more disconsolate people back in Jerusalem, seven miles back along the road.

## They are re-energised

At first their hearts were burning, now their hearts are bursting. They couldn't wait to finish supper, they can't rest – they jump up from the table. No matter how late the hour, they've become burning incendiaries with hope restored, perspective changed, spirits energised, and they rise up immediately, 'They got up and returned at once to Jerusalem' (v33, NIV). By the way they tell the news to the Eleven in Jerusalem, it's obvious that they were excited. I can imagine them not walking back to Jerusalem, but excitedly running, leaping, laughing and shouting 'He's alive!'.

Something incredible has happened in them. They are carried with hope, transported by joy – all is not lost after all. They go to tell their story to others, 'and found the eleven and those *who were* with them gathered together, saying, "The Lord is risen ...", And they told about the things *that had happened* on the road, and how He was known to them in the breaking of bread' (vv33–35). Two disconsolate disciples whose lives had been on a downward spiral just a few hours ago, are transformed by the power and presence of Jesus in the process of journey. That's the joy of journey that God has for you.

Jesus is the centre of this story. He came alongside us at the cross, forgave our sin and guilt, but didn't leave us there. He set us on a journey, 'coming alongside' others with the grace and truth He's imparted to us. This is the Jesus model. If there are 100 people in your church, each following the Jesus model of journeying with two other people, and every person in your church is taking this to heart, every week it could be journeying with 200 people.

If each one of those two people was a non-churched person, from Monday to Saturday *paraclesis* will be working out into the world. Coming alongside and letting Jesus be who He is to us and through us, as we connect our story to their story with God's story. We would see radical change as people come to know Christ. May God quicken to your heart the possibility and potential of your journey and life experience. After reading this book you can never again say that you've nothing to bring to someone else's life. You have your own resource of journey, and a model for journeying – Jesus style.

CHAPTER 8

# Choose life

'like a father with his children, we exhorted
[*parakaleo*] each one of you and encouraged you
and charged you to lead a life worthy of God.'
(1 Thess. 2:11–12, RSV)

If there's one thing needed for the journey, its clear direction. Often we hear someone say, 'He's lost his sense of direction', or, 'If only I had some kind of direction on this.' Direction is to do with decisions and choices. It's the power of choice that enables us to chart the course and direction of our lives. The choice to follow Christ through repentance and forgiveness at the cross brought new direction to our lives. A new road opened up before us and a new journey began as we entered the bigger redemption story. 'Let us look to Jesus, the author and finisher of our faith, who for the joy that was set before Him endured the cross, despising the shame, and is seated at the right hand of the throne of God' (Heb. 12:2, MEV).

## Spiritual direction

The next facet then of the *paraclesis* diamond is 'to exhort'. Paul says to the Thessalonians, 'like a father with his children we exhorted [*parakaleo*] each one of you and encouraged you and charged you to lead a life worthy of God' (1 Thess. 2:11–12, RSV). Paul expresses a father's heart, exhorting, directing them to 'lead a life worthy of God'. This somewhat old-fashioned sounding Bible word – exhort – means to direct, guide, advise, recommend or warn. It means bringing spiritual direction. We exhort someone to do something, follow an action, make a decision, take a choice, or move in a direction.

People at times lose their way on the journey. There are points along the way where they need guidance, insight, wisdom and direction. Spiritual direction focuses on developing wise life choices that shape behaviour patterns and life outcomes. 'I myself am convinced, my brothers and sisters, that you yourselves are full of goodness, filled with knowledge and competent to instruct one another' (Rom. 15:14, NIV).

## A rope around your ankle

In Deuteronomy 30:19 Moses exhorts the Israelites to 'choose life', and that's spiritual direction. Having being stuck in the wilderness for forty years he points them in the direction of the promised land and exhorts, 'I have set before you life and death, blessing and cursing; therefore choose life'. Life always has crossroads, junctions, intersections with different directions and destinations. C.S. Lewis said, 'One road leads home but thousands lead into the wilderness.'[1] Our decisions will determine the road we take and the direction we choose will determine our destiny, it's fundamental to the journey.

I once read about circus elephants being trained by attaching a long heavy chain and collar around the ankle of its rear leg, then the chain was attached to an iron stake. Day after day, hour, after hour the young elephant struggles to break free from its powerful grip. After many months of futile efforts it realises escape is impossible. Eventually relinquishing its struggle to be free, it surrenders. Having accepted its fate it becomes compliant and docile, getting used to the collar round its ankle. After finally giving up trying, its masters remove the giant chain and collar replacing it with a smaller, lighter rope. By this time all the fight has gone; the elephant has adjusted, becoming accustomed to the lighter weight of a rope. After a while the rope is detached from the stake without the elephant realising it, and is replaced by an unattached ring of rope around its ankle and the conditioning is complete.

That small ring of rope becomes the power holding it captive. If it ever opened its eyes to the reality, the truth is it could choose to walk away at any moment. That moment of realisation would change its direction. Since the elephant doesn't know, it doesn't make the choice to take the step to freedom. So, many years later, it remains bound by something it's conditioned by. If, like Nellie, it realised it was not chained, it would pack its trunk and say goodbye to the circus.

The problem is that the elephant is living in a state of what is called 'learned helplessness'. And that's how it can be in people's lives. Thank God that, at the cross, the chains of sin are broken. But some continue to live life with a rope around their ankle dictating the choices they make, the directions they take, living in the same old familiar patterns they've become conditioned to during life. Journeying together with them will enable them to face the reality of those old familiar patterns and life choices.

## Three-dimensional living

Jesus continually talked about life. However, three different Greek words are used to describe it. If we're to bring spiritual direction to people's lives, it's important to understand the three dimensions of living Jesus talks about. The first, in Luke 8:14, is about a farmer sowing seeds: 'And the ones *that* fell among thorns are those who, when they have heard, go out and are choked with cares, riches and pleasures of life [*bios*]'. The Greek word *bios* refers to our external world, our outer life, our manner of living in this world, how we live and do life day by day – our lifestyle, the way we choose to live. The 'cares' are the anxieties, worries, commitments, responsibilities, constant pressures and demands of everyday life. Jesus says the cares, riches, and pleasures of this *bios* wrap themselves around us like weeds throttling, choking us to death. They hold us back, like the rope around the ankle.

We live life at such a busy pace, juggling mobile phones, texting, emailing, calling, tweeting, networking. Our world gets so full and life so busy. We are swept along by the busy-busy syndrome; caught up in the grip of hurry-hurry sickness; the world of rush-rush-rush. The in-tray of life never empties, there are never enough hours in the day, never enough time to get it all done. Everyone wants everything yesterday. We are caught up in the hamster wheel of daily existence and ever-frequent activity. We become workaholics, consumed by the significance of our own activity, driven people living with stress, anxiety, uncertainty, barely coping under the burden of busyness. It becomes a heavy rope around our ankle. Someone said, 'I'm not stressed out. I've just been in a very bad mood for 30 years.' The challenge in *bios* is one of choices and change. Journeying is taking time to understand the world of the *bios,* helping people to reorder lifestyle issues that are choking and strangling them to death.

Another aspect of life Jesus talked about is found in Luke 9:24: 'Whoever desires to save his life [*psuche*] will lose it, but whoever loses his life [*psuche*] for my sake will save it'. The Greek word *psuche* used here doesn't refer to the outer, but inner life. The inner world of thoughts, feelings, choices, decisions, our private, personal world is hidden from view. The inner motivations and personal agendas that influence and impact external behaviour patterns, choices and decisions shape the pattern of our lives. The burden of busyness leads to the weight of weariness. Under the load of cares, the traveller becomes weary on the journey.

Studies show that more often than not, the need to prove our worth and value and find a sense of significance, pushes us into the busy-busy syndrome. Always feeling the need to be needed, to please people and gain their approval. These subtle drives push us on to strive to do more.

Sometimes, through guilt, a fear of failure, not wanting to disappoint, or wanting to meet others' expectations, we push ourselves beyond our limits, taking on more than is good for us, extending ourselves almost to the point of exhaustion. The problem is that we can only live on adrenalin rushes for a certain amount of time. The highs and lows drain us of emotional energy and our drivenness leads to exhaustion. With restlessness and unease in our soul, the weight of weariness takes its toll and life becomes a duty, not a delight.

The third aspect of life Jesus talked about is the Greek word *zoe*. He said, 'I am way, the truth and the life [*zoe*]' (John 14:6). It's the word Jesus used frequently. Greek lexicons tell us it means God's kind of life, the source of all life. Not *bios* life, or *psuche* life, but *zoe*: life as it can only be found in God, life out of which creation sprang, the foundation and fount of all life. 'In the beginning was the Word and the Word was with God, and the Word was God … In Him was life [*zoe*] and that life [*zoe*] was the light of men' (John 1:1,4); 'The thief does not come except to steal, and to kill, and to destroy. I have come that they may have life [*zoe*], and that they may have *it* more abundantly' (John 10:10).

When people struggle with the burden of busyness and the weight of weariness they become spiritually drained, depleted and burnt out. Burnout is a spiritual condition. It's like driving a car with a burnt out clutch – the engine's running but the gears won't engage, the clutch just keeps spinning fast, burning out and going nowhere. Like coming to the well when the well has run dry, saying and doing the right things, but with nothing to draw on to keep you going. Living with a rope around the ankle.

Journeying is not just a matter of helping people reorder their external world, although that's part of it. The answer is not just rearranging and reorganising the *bios*. That's about as useful as rearranging deck chairs on the *Titanic*. No matter how well you do it, the ship will go down anyway. We need to help people recognise what is going on in their *bios*, understand how it relates to their *psuche*, realising their outer world only reflects the struggle of their inner world. Then bring the spiritual direction to choose life, God's kind of life.

## Do you want to change?

One day Jesus' journey brought Him to a man by a pool: 'Now a certain man was there who had an infirmity thirty-eight years' (John 5:5). It was by the sheep gate into Jerusalem, where sheep were taken to cattle market, a noisy busy place with thousands of sheep wandering everywhere, bleating and milling. Sheep traders buying, selling, bartering, would wash sheep in the pool before market. It was smelly, dirty, murky, contaminated, polluted by sheep – an unhealthy, unpleasant environment. Also, 'a great multitude of sick people, blind, lame, paralysed' were waiting (John 5:3). Thousands of sick people crowded around five arches with disease, pain and misery everywhere.

They were there because things could change any minute. Once in a while an angel stirred the water and the first one in would be healed. The constant question was, would an angel visit today? Will there be anyone to put me in? Will I be first? Will I or won't I get into the pool? There was an ever-present uncertainty, a competitive edginess of continual underlying anxiety as every day hundreds, if not thousands, vied for their opportunity to get near the pool. If the water moved slightly there was pandemonium, the ruthless crowd surged forward, all banking on getting in. It was first come, first served. The vast crowd would compete, pushing, shoving, every man for himself, like a Boxing Day sale – arms, legs, elbows flying everywhere. Don't worry about others, just fight to get yourself in first. It was a daily battle not to lose your place in the pecking order.

Daily this man lived with this constant hustle and bustle, the busy cut and thrust of life around him, the underlying atmosphere of misery, anxiety, competitiveness and uncertainty. Hoping every day his turn will come, his world would change, the waters would move and he would get in, only to be disappointed at the end of the day. Jesus comes to where he is, surrounded by unease and edginess, living by this pool of disappointment.

Now, you'd think Jesus would heal this man, but the Bible doesn't say that. He didn't even pray for him, or offer to help him into the water.

What seems unusual on this occasion is that Jesus asks him a question, 'Do you want to be made well?' (John 5:6). You would think this was a foregone conclusion. In doing so Jesus is presenting him with a choice. Jesus recognised that the man may not have wanted to, and respected his power of choice. Jesus wasn't blaming him by asking the question. Matthew Henry's commentary puts it like this: 'He asked him, *Wilt thou be made whole?* A strange question to be asked one that had been so long ill. Some indeed would not be made whole, because their sores serve them to beg by and serve them for an excuse for idleness.'[2]

It's a simple yes or no question: 'do you want your world to change; do you want this circumstance to be different?' You'd think his immediate response after lying there such a long time would be, 'Yes, sir! I've been waiting for this day all of my life.' But he doesn't respond like that. He replies, 'Sir, I have no man to put me into the pool when the water is stirred up' (v7). In other words, 'Sir, you don't understand my problem. I'm waiting for the water to stir, but when it moves, there's nobody here to help me; I've no friends, even in this vast crowd, I'm here alone by myself in this.' He appears to blame others for his plight. It's their fault. His response reflects a sense of self-pity. He's feeling sorry for himself. I describe this as the PLM syndrome: 'poor little me'. You can almost hear the pain in his voice. Instead of responding, 'Yes, Lord', he responds, 'Lord, it can never change.'

Like the conditioned elephant, he had become resigned to his circumstance – learned helplessness. He had accepted his lot in life, that nothing will change for him. Verse 7 says, 'while I am coming, another steps down before me'. There's always someone quicker than me, so I'm stuck here, caught in a freeze-frame. Something pushed the pause button of life, and I've accepted my lot. He's settled for a victim mentality: 'I am the victim, other people did stuff to me, things have happened I had no control over, my life is on hold. I'm simply a victim of circumstances.' The issue is not that the man by the pool had been a victim – there was no denying that – but that he had settled for a victim mentality. *A victim mentality means we consistently look for reasons why life isn't working for us*. The presence of Jesus meant that despite life dealing him a terrible hand, he had the possibility of moving from being a victim to becoming a victor and moving on with his life.

## The challenge of choice

When we journey alongside people, very often the circumstances and struggle have been so long, their journey so hard, there's a passive, 'it'll never change, I can't do anything about it' attitude. It is what I now describe as 'the rope around the ankle'. Journeying is helping them to begin to understand and face that. It is saying, 'Hang on a minute, things can change.'

Jesus exhorts the man with a clear directive to change, to 'choose life'. 'Then Jesus said to him, Get up! Pick up your mat and walk' (v8, NIV). Jesus doesn't walk away, leaving him in his self-pity. *Paraclesis* is helping people move on from where they're often stuck in life, journeying with them out of that situation. Jesus directed him to pick up his mat by himself and 'walk'. Sometimes people have an expectation of being carried, but journeying isn't carrying, it's walking with someone. I want you to take responsibility for your world, *bios*, *psuche* and *zoe*. This is a huge challenge people often face, the reason they need someone journeying with them is because on their own they can't face and deal with that kind of challenge.

The fact of the matter is that we don't always choose what happens in life. Some things we have no control over. We didn't choose to be born, or choose our parents; there are many things in life we don't choose. We didn't choose the way someone wounded or hurt us. However, we do have the freedom to choose what we do with it. Dr William Glasser, a psychologist and psychiatrist, points out in his book *Reality Therapy*[3] that if people are going to find help, they must first face reality. Then he introduces what he calls his second 'R': Responsibility. He says we may not have chosen what has happened to us (reality), but we can choose what we do with it now (responsibility). Jimmy Dean said, 'I can't change the direction of the wind, but I can adjust my sails to always reach my destination.'[4]

Viktor Frankl, Austrian neurologist, psychiatrist and author of bestselling book *Man's Search for Meaning*, was imprisoned by the Nazis in World War II because he was a Jew. His wife, children, and parents were all killed in the holocaust. The Gestapo made him strip. He stood there totally naked. As they cut away His wedding ring, Viktor said to himself, 'You can take my wife, you can take my children and parents, you can strip me of my clothes and freedom, but there's one thing no person can ever take away from me and that's my freedom to choose how I react to what happens to me!'[5] Even under the most difficult of circumstances, how we respond, despite the sadness and pain, can transform a tragedy into a turning point.

The journey of life is a series of choices. Every day is largely a process of our choices, and what we choose largely defines us. We choose our cars, houses, friends, jobs, spouses. We choose to live the way we do, and those choices become what we repeatedly do. Because we're responsible for our choices, the key is taking control of them.

The loss of felt choice is not the loss of real choice. The elephant didn't understand that. It's the loss of felt choice that produces a victim mentality and we become creatures of habit. Habit is the unconscious loss of felt choice, when we lose the awareness we are choosing beings and function on autopilot. We cannot change what we will not acknowledge. Lao Tzu said, 'If you do not change direction, you will end up where you are now heading.'[6]

The most empowering thing is waking up every morning with the realisation that we can 'choose life' today. To know that instead of continuing on doing the same old, same old, we choose to make changes. We don't have to live with a rope around our ankle. Things can be different. Waking up each morning recognising I can draw on an abundant supply of *zoe* life, choosing to allow God's life to affect my *psuche* and *bios*, because God always meets us at the point of choice. 'Walk in the Spirit, and you shall not fulfil the lust of the flesh' (Gal. 5:16).

## The consequence of choice

Choices are consequential by design or by default. When we choose a behaviour we choose its consequences. Steven Covey said, 'While we are free to choose our actions, we are not free to choose the consequences of our actions.'[7] Make no mistake, the choices we make today have enormous impact on life tomorrow. Sometimes people we come alongside are living with the consequence of a bad choice, and we need to help them face responsibility, and find fresh direction and insight. Maybe they've lost the sense of their ability to make choices, or lost confidence in their own ability to make choices. They need someone journeying with them, helping them find their confidence in God to make choices according to His plans and purposes.

Jesus gives the man a further exhortation. Not only to stand up and walk, but to change his direction. He says, 'you have been made well. Sin no more, lest a worse thing come upon you' (John 5:14). The text suggests he's there because a wrong choice got him there in the first place. It is as though Jesus said, 'go and don't do it any more, otherwise you'll be in an even worse place. I am exhorting you, giving you spiritual direction – you have made the choice to stand, now continue making right choices as you journey forward, choosing the right directions, the right pathway, choosing the God kind of life.' That's the wonderful message of the gospel – we can choose to live God's kind of life.

## Pitiful or powerful?

The time had come for this man to get up and do something special with his life. With a victim mentality he was pitiful. Jesus turned pitifulness into powerfulness. How? By the man taking his God-given power of choice, standing up, picking up his mat and walking forward in a new direction. Journeying is helping people pick up their mat and walk, to take the rope of a victim mentality off the ankle, then putting one foot in front of the other, one step at a time, to journey forward.

This man was pitiful but became powerful. Being powerful is not what we achieve, it is what we choose. That's the wonderful joy of *paraclesis*, helping people take back control of choice. Journeying with someone through that enabling process, exhorting, bringing spiritual direction to 'choose life' – to live life well, not unwell.

## CHAPTER 9

# Strong at the broken places

'We who are strong ought to bear the weaknesses of the weak and not please ourselves.'
(Rom. 15:1–2, MEV)

Journeying is the strong bearing the infirmities of the weak. Ernest Hemingway, in *A Farewell to Arms*, wrote the line, 'The world breaks everyone and afterward many are strong at the broken places.'[1]

Hemingway, an ambulance driver in World War I, was wounded when a shell exploded near him and shrapnel ripped through his leg, which was almost lost. Nursed back to health, he was forever changed by war.

On the journey of life there are broken places, and the facet of the *paraclesis* diamond (as described in Chapter 2) relating to this is 'comfort': 'So comfort [*parakaleo*] each other and make each other strong' (1 Thess. 5:11, NLV). Today comfort generally means soothe, reassure, give sympathy, make comfortable, bring relief. But the word used for *paraclesis* has a much richer and fuller meaning. Coming from the Latin word *confortare* – 'to strengthen' – *con* means 'with' and *fortare* means 'fortitude' or 'strength', meaning 'to bring strength', to build up, restore and repair. Helping someone in a broken place to find healing, wholeness and recovery, enabling them to be brave and courageous in rebuilding their lives and moving on from a position of strength, not weakness.

It's Sunday morning, and a guest speaker is in church. A lady makes her way to the service to hear Him – she's a regular attender. As the guest in the pulpit begins to speak His eyes fell on this woman at the back. She's a pitiful sight, bent double, her hands almost touching the ground. She shuffled and hobbled into church as usual this morning. He calls her forward and she stumbles her way to the front, only recognising who's in church by their feet. She crouches in front of Him – a deformed, distorted, crippled, bundle of humanity.

It started 18 years earlier, probably with back pain. In order to alleviate and ease the pain she'd lean slightly forward until eventually over time she is now bent almost double. When she tries to straighten up a knot of muscle in her back stops her where the spine has fused and locked her into a fixed position. Today the condition is known as Ankylosing Spondylitis, also called the Marie-Strümpell disease, which is a kind of arthritic condition that deteriorates the body over the years. According to the *Merck Manual of Diagnosis and Therapy*[2] it's a chronic progressive ossification of the joints, especially the lower spine. 'There was a woman present, so twisted and bent over with arthritis that she couldn't even look up' (Luke 13:11, MSG). She is trapped in this physical condition. Now this Sabbath morning she finds herself here in front of Jesus.

## An infirm spirit

Dr Luke tells us she not only has a curvature of the spine, but a crippling in her spirit; she 'had a spirit of infirmity [for] eighteen years' (v11). He says Jesus spoke to her, touched her and freed her 'from [her] infirmity'. This word 'infirmity' is interesting. The Greek word for strength is *sthenes*, and for *infirmity*, is *asthenes*, the opposite – weakness. When an 'a' is placed in front of a Greek word it turns it from positive to negative, or the opposite. If 'a' is put in front of 'theist', you have 'atheist'. The word 'infirmity' – *asthenes* – means lacking in strength, or weakness. Dr Luke relates her external deformity to an internal infirmity. A physical affliction with a spiritual connection. Dr Luke, with his medical and spiritual eyes, looks beyond what he sees outwardly, her deformity, and sees something deeper, her infirmity.

Some commentators postulate she was demon possessed but the narrative doesn't suggest that. Jesus always spoke to demons, whereas here He spoke to the woman. Jesus never laid hands on the demon possessed, but He did this woman. Demons always reacted in His presence, but there is no reaction or outburst here. Demons called out in His presence unless commanded by Him to keep quiet. He does not address or rebuke the devil or demons. The Greek word for demon possession, *daimonizomai*, isn't found in this passage. She is described as a woman 'whom Satan has bound' (v16). Bound in the Greek, *deó* means to bind, tie, or tether. Jesus then says that she was 'loosed from this bond' (v16). The Greek for 'to loose' is *apolyo*. So we have here bound and loosed, not possessed and delivered.

*Apolyo* means to loose bonds that tie, or to untie, free or release. It was also used as a medical term describing binding bandages to dress a wound, and even today we talk about binding up a wound. Here, Dr Luke uses it. In fact, when Jesus raised Lazarus from the dead, Jesus uses exactly the same words. When Lazarus emerges from the tomb covered in graveclothes and wrapped in cloth, Jesus turned to His disciples and said, 'Loose [*apolyo*] him, and let him go' (John 11:44). The Amplified version puts it, 'his hands and feet *tightly* wrapped in burial cloths (linen strips), and with a [burial] cloth wrapped around his face. Jesus said to them, "Unwrap him and release him."' Take off the bandages so he not only has life, but liberty.

## A human struggle

Often on life's journey people struggle with human frailty and infirmity. Things happen that wound and weaken. Unfortunately, some never seem to recover from battering and bruising blows that strike them deeply. Their hearts still reel and bleed from deep wounds of hurt, horror and hatred. They travel through life as walking wounded, patched up and bandaged like wounded war veterans, with the war continuing to rage inside them long after the battle has ended. Along life's pathway their spirit has been damaged. At best they can wrap bandages around their wounds, all kinds of bandages, through what they pursue in life, how they relate in life, or lifestyles they create to compensate in trying to deal with their own wounds. As you listen, often underneath, seeping through the bandages, is a running sore, an open wound, an infirm spirit. Something happened at a broken place.

Exploring this some years ago I came across the fascinating word *psychosomatic*, coming from two Greek words, *psuche* or *psyche* for the soul or inner life, and *soma* for the body. I stumbled into the world of infirmities and their psychosomatic impact, which is the theory that the human spirit has a direct impact on the mind and body. When I first came to faith I was taught about sin and sickness, where you needed forgiveness and healing respectively, but no one talked to me about the world of 'infirmities', where things deeply wounding our spirits have significant impact in our bodies and behaviours.

A book that helped me was *None of These Diseases* by Dr I. McMillen revised and updated by his grandson Dr David Stern, both Christian medics. In it they talk about holding things in our spirit: anger, guilt, hatred, fear, stress, resentment, bitterness. These are not just emotions but spiritual dynamics that actually release chemicals into the bloodstream and nervous system – neurotransmitters that convey messages into our bloodstream, prompting physiological and psychological reactions.

There are no built-in shock absorbers in the human spirit that absorb anger, guilt, hatred, fear, stress, resentment, unforgiveness and bitterness. We were never created to carry them in our spirits – they're unnatural impositions in the human spirit, which can't contain them. A wounded spirit throws them off into the rest of our system and that's what psychosomatic means. Read Proverbs 18:14: 'The spirit of a man will sustain him in sickness, but who can bear a broken spirit?' The answer is no one, we're not created to bear a wounded spirit. We're created with spirits to sustain us in sickness. But the text says a broken spirit, an infirmed spirit, is *un*-bearable, *dis*-abling, causing *dis*-ease.

Something crippling had happened in this woman's spirit that impacted her body. Dr Luke links her physical condition to a spiritual origin rather than an organic or physical cause. J.B. Phillips' translation puts it, 'a woman who for eighteen years had been ill from some psychological cause; she was bent double and was quite unable to straighten herself up ' (Luke 13:11). Her condition came to define her.

## Beneath the waterline

Human beings, like icebergs, only reveal the tip. Often other things go on beneath the waterline. Isaiah 11:3, speaking of Jesus, says, 'he shall not judge by the sight of his eyes, Nor decide by the hearing of his ears'. To the Pharisees He said, 'you are like whitewashed tombs which indeed appear beautiful outwardly, but inside are full of dead *men's* bones and all uncleanness' (Matt. 23:27). Dr Luke saw this woman's condition beneath the waterline. Life is never as simple as it seems – human experience always runs deep. Our lives are always multi-layered. All behaviour has physical, psychological or spiritual causes. Nothing is created in a vacuum. Journeying with people is recognising that often, beneath the waterline of outward behaviours, is a wounded spirit. Often in church we've not taken time to understand this, but have simply offered superficial platitudes.

This was true of the prophets and priests of Israel: 'from the prophet even to the priest, everyone deals falsely. They have also healed the hurt of my people slightly, saying, "Peace, peace!" When *there is* no peace' (Jer. 6:13–14). This word, shalom, is wellness, wholeness, completeness. Here's the indictment by Jeremiah, that in God's house, where this woman was, they declared the message of wholeness but hadn't delivered healing. They'd said 'Peace, peace', but had only healed the hurts of the people slightly. One translation of verse 14 puts it, 'They act as if my people's wounds were only scratches. "All is well," they say, "when all is not well"' (GNT). Another one says, 'They treat my people's wounds as though they were not serious, saying, "Everything is alright!" But it's not alright' (GW). But on this Sabbath day in God's House it was all about to change for this woman. Jesus would put it right.

## Broken places

Stuff happens along life's highway. Life gets fractured, damaged and broken. There are broken places where people fall by the wayside. Broken relationships: my estimation would be that ninety-five per cent of all non-physical issues have a strong relational component. Broken and damaged at the point of a relationship: family, marriage, childhood, peers, friends, church, colleagues. People hurt; that's a fact of life. Broken dreams: hopes and aspirations dashed. People who were promised so much but others who delivered so little. People with unachieved goals, unrealised expectations, who thought life would turn out a particular way but something happened – promises were broken, dreams shattered, hopes unfulfilled. Broken hearts: the loss of a loved one, bereavement, maybe a miscarriage, or childlessness, maybe unrequited love. Even jilted or betrayed in marriage or divorce; maybe abortion, sorrow, grief and sadness. A broken image: identity and self-image broken and marred. A badly damaged sense of self-worth and low self-esteem. Through psychological, verbal, emotional impact. Bullied, humiliated, ridiculed, denigrated, rejected by others. Put down by parents, peers, teachers, siblings.

Broken cisterns: 'For My people have committed a double evil: They have abandoned Me, the fountain of living water, and dug cisterns for themselves, cracked cisterns that cannot hold water' (Jer. 2:13, HCSB). A cistern was a big tank cut in the rock to hold water but often the rock cracked and the water seeped out. It would drain away, leaving mud and sludge at the bottom. Where they thought they'd find fresh water, they found themselves wallowing in mud and sludge.

How many cisterns have people drunk at that don't satisfy? Broken at a failing watering hole – they thought it would satisfy their deepest longings, only to find moral failure, losing their moral compass. Ethically losing their integrity, financially losing their sense of honesty, lying and cheating. Maybe caught up in pornography, losing virtue and purity. These are broken cisterns that never satisfy, ending up wallowing in mud and filth at the bottom. Drinking the dregs of the bitter waters of the guilt and shame. Broken body: bodily afflictions. Physical and congenital disease and deformity. Disability, physical abuse, sexual abuse, longstanding severe illness, incurable disease and injury.

There are many in our congregations who understand these broken places, they were part of their own journey. They have an awareness and understanding of what goes unrecognised beneath the water line. This is their resource of journey, redeemed and restored by grace, truth and the power of Christ.

## A wounded spirit

The common denominator threading through all these broken places is deep pain deposited into the human spirit. Broken places are painful places. Arthur Janov highlighted the concept of 'the pool pain' some years ago. He described pain as a dominant, powerful, negative force in the personality, generating strong destructive feelings, psychological reactions and behaviour patterns. Pain in a wounded spirit has a deep and profound impact. How we process our pool of pain influences the course of our journey. The pain of disappointment, personal pain, relational pain, the pain of loss, of humiliation, shame, rejection, guilt and regret, are seriously debilitating.

Follow the link here: a broken place produces a wounded spirit that carries a pool of pain. People think pain and hurt can be healed but it can't. It's a symptom not the cause. Pain in the body simply tells us something is wrong. Spiritual pain is a consequence of a wounded spirit and when there's a wounded spirit, we look for bandages and balm to ease the pain. People wrap bandages round their lives, trying to ease their pain through all kinds of life patterns. However, when a wounded spirit is healed, then pain dissolves, bandages are discarded and behaviour changes.

For a wounded spirit to be healed and not remain it needs to become a scar. Where there is a scar, healing has taken place. Many living with a wounded spirit do so because no one's journeyed with them, helping them process the pain of the wound until it becomes a scar. Journeying is walking with someone until the wound becomes a scar. Like the disciples with Lazarus, slowly, gently, patiently and with great understanding and grace, taking off the bandages that have bound the wound for so long.

Paul describes his infirmity as a 'thorn in the flesh' (2 Cor. 12:7). A thorn in the flesh means a wound, pain and poison in our system. Wanting to be free from the pain, he asks God three times to deliver him. Each time God replied, 'My grace is sufficient for you' (2 Cor. 12:9). Instead of reacting negatively to the pain, he responds to God's grace, receiving and embracing it, declaring, 'gladly I will rather boast in my infirmities, that the power of Christ may rest upon me' (2 Cor. 12:9). His receipt of grace turned his wound into a grace scar. We can choose to respond to grace because God's 'grace is sufficient'. He promises to supply a corresponding source of grace for every life circumstance.

It's possible to react to the circumstance and fail to respond to God's grace. The writer to the Hebrews warns us to be careful of this. 'Be careful that none of you fails to respond to the grace which God gives, for if he does there can very easily spring up in him a bitter spirit which is not only bad in itself but can also poison the lives of many others' (Heb. 12:15, J.B. Phillips). Notice he says if we don't respond to God's grace, a wounded, bitter spirit poisons not only our life, but the lives of those around us. A bitter spirit is toxic and if we don't deal with it, we become toxic, a root of bitterness takes hold and we become a victim of our broken place. If we live as victims we will become agents of pain, victimising others. It works like this: I get hurt, so I hurt you, make you feel the same pain as me and make you as miserable as I am. Someone criticises me, so I criticise back. I project my bitterness on to them. I am wounded, so I will wound you and make you suffer for my pain.

## The wounded healer

That's not to condemn people, God only knows what they've suffered in their life. We're there to support, love and understand them, bringing strength and grace. Grace is the antidote to the bitter poison in the system of the soul. Holding bitterness and resentment in our wounded spirit is like drinking poison and waiting for the other person to die. Unforgiveness and bitterness binds and incarcerates the human spirit. It's 'poison'.

Forgiveness is a key part of grace, and we can choose the pathway of forgiveness: 'Bear with each other and forgive one another if any of you has a grievance against someone. Forgive as the Lord forgave you' (Col. 3:13, NIV). Journeying is helping people to realise fully God's forgiveness, His goodness towards them, enabling them to receive an overwhelming sense of God's forgiveness for them. It is out of that strength they'll be able to reach out and forgive others. Forgiving as we have been forgiven sets us free from our past, heals our wounds, releases our pain and makes us strong again at the broken place. Forgiveness is choosing to let go and choosing to embrace grace. Forgiveness turns pain into a grace scar.

In the words of Proverbs we ask, 'a wounded spirit who can bear?' (Prov. 18:14, KJV). The gospel responds: only Jesus, the wounded healer. 'He *was* wounded for our transgressions, *He was* bruised for our iniquities' (Isa. 53:5). We have a High Priest, 'touched with the feeling of our infirmities [*asthenes*]' (Heb. 4:15, KJV), the pain and hurt of our wounding. If we want to understand wounding and scars we must turn again to an old Roman gibbet, a rugged cross. There are wounds and pain here. Medics tell us there are five types of wounds. Bruising, piercing, tearing, grazing and penetration by a sharp instrument. On the cross Jesus suffered all of those types of wounds literally in His own body. The risen Christ is the wounded healer with scars. Scars on His back like a ploughed field where He was lacerated. Scars on His brow where a crown of thorns was forced on His head. A scar in His side where Roman soldiers stabbed Him and blood and water flowed out. Scars on

His nail-pierced feet and hands. The message of the cross is that God not only saves us and forgives our sin but that He heals the wounded soul.

When we come to Him in our pain and woundedness, willing to take off our bandages, the wounded healer touches us with His nail-scarred hands, healing our wounds, making them scars. Then as we journey with others, we can help them take off their bandages, allowing the healing balm of Gilead to flow through us to them. This is *paraclesis* at work, bringing comfort, strength and healing from God. Journeying alongside others with their broken places, wounds and pain all the way back to the cross. It's there, as we gaze on His marred features, that we're overwhelmed with awe, lost in wonder, love and praise. It's there in His presence that we're made strong at the broken places. God calls us to be such a healing community.

## Loosed and lifted

As the woman with her infirmity crouches in front of Jesus in the Synagogue, she hears the Master's voice speaking words of freedom to her soul, and something breaks inside her spirit as He says, 'Woman, you are loosed from your infirmity' (Luke 13:12). In a moment, He looses her, eighteen years of pain inflicted by Satan is dissolved in an instant, then 'he laid *his* hands on her, and immediately she was made straight' (Luke 13:13). His hands of grace, His hands of mercy, His hands of love, His hands of healing. He touches her, pouring strength into this pitiful body, and healing and wholeness flows into her crippled spirit. She stood straight for the first time in years. Suddenly, instead of looking at those beautiful feet of Jesus, she lifts her head, looks into the most wonderful eyes she's ever seen in all her life. This infirm woman is loosed and lifted.

I'm reminded of the words of hymn writer Bill Gaither:

Shackled by a heavy burden
'Neath a load of guilt and shame
Then the hand of Jesus touched me
Now I am no longer the same
He touched me, He touched me
And Oh the joy that filled my soul,
Something happened and now I know,
He touched me and made me whole.'

Normal church was suspended. I doubt they got to hear the guest speaker that morning as the place erupted with an immediate praise meeting in the temple and the woman 'glorified God' (v13). She journeyed out of the Synagogue that day walking tall, a transformed woman. Not only a woman physically healed but whose spirit was released and made whole through the power and presence of Jesus. People don't have to be bound by the crippling wounds of the past or live with the pain of the present. They don't have to live at a broken place, they can be liberated and set free in Jesus' name. And that's the joy of journeying – *Paraclesis* at work.

## CHAPTER 10

# Another Helper

'I will ask My Father, and He will give you another Helper [*parakletos*]. He will be with you forever.' (John 14:16, NLV)

We look again to the *paraclesis* diamond and come to another facet, *parakletos*. When we journey with others we're not left to our own devices, simply relying on a basic set of helping skills. Before returning to His Father, Jesus reassures His disciples that the Father will send them 'another Helper' – *parakletos* – to be alongside them in Jesus' place. In the temple Simeon received the coming of the consolation [*paraklesis*] of Israel in Jesus. Jesus, now returning to His Father, promises to send 'another Helper' [*parakletos*] as His successor.

Jesus had been at the disciples' side for three years, walking, talking and journeying with them, teaching, leading, guiding and discipling them. Now they'd have another Helper, one just like Him, to be with them, ministering to them as He had. He gives them His word that they'll not be left on their own but sent a supernatural Helper from heaven. 'Nevertheless I tell you the truth; It is to your advantage that I go away; for if I do not go away, the Helper [*parakletos*] will not come to you; but if I depart, I will send Him to you' (John 16:7). The Holy Spirit would be to them all Jesus had been and more. They would do even greater things than He'd done through the Spirit's enabling. 'The person who trusts me will not only do what I'm doing but even greater things, because I, on my way to the Father, am giving you the same work to do that I've been doing. You can count on it' (John 14:12, MSG).

## A person, not an impersonal influence

The word 'another', written in John 14:16, doesn't mean another of a *different* kind – *heteros* in the Greek – but another *of the same kind* – *allos* in the Greek. In other words, Jesus promises the coming Helper and Comforter will be exactly the same kind of person, powerfully fulfilling His ministry in a number of ways.

Jesus refers to the Holy Spirit as the *parakletos* on four occasions in John's Gospel. Some commentators have designated the term *paraklete* as a title or name of the Holy Spirit, but actually Jesus doesn't use *parakletos* as a title of office but as a description of function and operation. In fact, when Jesus speaks of the Holy Spirit's ministry He uses four prepositions. In school we learned a preposition precedes a proposition, in other words a preposition directly relates to a purpose. The four prepositions Jesus uses are, He will be 'with you', He will be 'in you', He will come 'upon you', and He will 'flow out' of you, but for what purposes? An understanding of these purposes enables us to see how the Holy Spirit enables us in journeying with others.

The *Star Wars* movies made famous the oft repeated line, 'May the Force be with you'. Some people view the Holy Spirit in this way, as some kind of invisible energy, an impersonal influence or vague impression. But Jesus describes the Holy Spirit not as an abstract 'It', but 'He', a real person, the third member of the Trinity having equality in the Godhead, possessing all the attributes of deity. He's eternally defined as God, omniscient, omnipresent, omnipotent, all-powerful, all-present, and all-knowing, co-equal, co-existent, and co-eternal with the Father and the Son. The disciples were commissioned 'in the name of the Father and of the Son and of the Holy Spirit' (Matt 28:19). The Holy Spirit was sent by Jesus from the Father to come alongside as we journey with others.

## He will be 'with you'

Jesus' first preposition is categorical, He will be 'with you', the one who comes alongside you, which is so fundamental to journeying. 'I will pray the Father, and He will give you another Helper [*parakletos*] … the Spirit of truth, whom the world cannot receive, because it neither sees him nor knows Him; but you know Him–for He dwells with you' (John 14:16–17).

Believe me, we're not left alone to our own devices in this task – we've been sent a supernatural Helper to be with us. What is His purpose in being 'with us'? Jesus gave us the clue: 'if I do not go away, the Helper [*parakletos*] will not come … And when He has come, He will convict the world of sin, and of righteousness, and of judgment' (John 16:7–8). He is with us to bring conviction to our lives. Conviction means the acute conscious awareness that something isn't right that all is not well with our soul, an inner realisation of guilt. The Greek word for sin here is *harmartia*, meaning to miss the mark, to go wrong and do wrong, to be mistaken, and miss or wander from the path.

Bringing this awareness to our lives is a work of the Holy Spirit. The fact of the matter is the Holy Spirit was convicting us before we ever came to know Jesus, bringing deep awareness of our need, and revealing the true condition of our souls before a Holy God. The realisation that we were wayward like sheep gone astray, each having turned to our own way (Isa. 53:6), that we were needy and impoverished before God. The Holy Spirit introduced us to the claims of Christ, convincing us that our need could only be met in Him. The Holy Spirit always points to Jesus, He is Christ's representative in every sense.

The Holy Spirit's convicting power continues after conversion, convincing us of the righteousness of Christ and so exposing our own pathways of unrighteousness. He doesn't drive us away from God but draws us near to the cross, where all unrighteousness is atoned for, where cleansing and redemption flow like a river to a penitent heart. Our consciences are cleansed and made alive to God by the Holy Spirit, giving us a spiritual compass for the journey of life. The Holy Spirit is with us, shining the light on Jesus, bringing realisation that we've wandered from the pathway, and got it wrong or done wrong.

Righteousness means right standing before God, and Jesus makes that possible. He bore the condemnation and judgment of our sin in order that we can stand without condemnation in God's presence. The Holy Spirit doesn't come to judge or condemn us, but to convince us of what is right – righteousness. D.L. Moody said if a stick is crooked, lay a straight one alongside and the entire world will clearly see it's crooked.[1]

The Holy Spirit shows us what's right and righteous, and everything that is right and righteous is found in Jesus. He reveals Jesus, convincing us of our need for Him and His righteousness: 'when the Helper [parakletos] comes, whom I shall send to you from the Father ... He will testify of Me' (John 15:26). As the light of Christ's character is revealed and Jesus is exalted and lifted up, the darkness of sin is exposed for what it is: independence from God and dependence on ourselves.

Be sure of this – conviction is not condemnation. Lingering, tormenting guilt and condemnation is not the work of the Holy Spirit, even if at times it seems as if such thoughts come from God. After all, we all have a conscience and know when we've done wrong and feel bad and guilty about it. Some people think the Holy Spirit watches them day and night, pointing out faults in their life. The Holy Spirit is never referred to as the judge, faultfinder, nitpicker, condemner or hyper-critic! He's not critical or condemnatory of us. It is sin that condemns, but Jesus who forgives.

This is why Paul said, 'There is therefore now no condemnation to those who are in Christ Jesus' (Rom. 8:1), so you can be sure that condemnation isn't the voice of the Holy Spirit. He doesn't condemn us for all that's wrong, but convinces us of all that is right in Jesus. We all have things we need to improve, but bringing guilt and shame on others does not help them to change.

Our role in journeying is not to make people feel guilty, but to allow the Holy Spirit to convince and convict people of the right pathway for them. This is His work, not ours. Righteousness is not only right standing with God but also with others. Righteousness is horizontal as well as vertical. It is through the work of the Spirit that broken relationships and right standing with others can be repaired and restored through the grace and forgiveness of Jesus. This is also part of journeying with others.

## He will be 'in you'

The second preposition Jesus used is, He will be 'in you'. 'He will give you another Helper [*parakletos*] ... but you know Him, for He dwells with you and will be in you' (John 14:16–17). The Holy Spirit is with you to convict, in you to convert. At conversion the Holy Spirit enters our lives to regenerate our spirits, bringing them into correspondence with God through salvation.

Jesus said to Nicodemus, 'Most assuredly, I say to you, unless one is born of water and the Spirit, he cannot enter the kingdom of God' (John 3:5–6). When we're born again by the Spirit of God, the Spirit indwells, changes, transforms and regenerates our lives through the power of Christ. We become living, walking, breathing temples in which He dwells. 'Or do you not know that your body is the temple of the Holy Spirit *who is* in you, whom you have from God ...?' (1 Cor. 6:19).

When the Holy Spirit takes up residence in us it's for the purpose of changing and conforming us into the likeness of Christ through the process of sanctification. 'God from the beginning chose you for salvation through sanctification by the Spirit and belief in the truth' (2 Thess. 2:13). Nothing can take the place of the Holy Spirit's work in the life of the believer. He ministers to the deepest needs of the human spirit, bringing with Him grace and truth, transforming our lives and personalities to become partakers of the nature of Christ. It is His indwelling ministry that brings about our growth into Christlikeness, making us more and more like Jesus.

Have you ever considered God's chief goal for your life? It is to mould you into the image of His Son, Jesus Christ. 'For from the very beginning God decided that those who came to him … should become like his Son' (Rom. 8:29, TLB), this is the work of the indwelling Spirit. He can only achieve it with our co-operation.

## His graces and gifts

The Spirit dwells in us in order to produce God's character in our lives in a way that cannot be achieved through human endeavour. Paul describes this outworking as 'the fruit of the Spirit' (Gal. 5:22), the nine character-graces exemplified in the life of Jesus. The Spirit's activity in our lives is to bring forth fruit and diffuse it in, and through our personality, the Christlike graces.

R.A. Torrey has expressed this fact with real spiritual insight: 'All real beauty of character, all real Christlikeness in us, is the Holy Spirit's work, it is His fruit. He bears it, not we … Settle it clearly and forever that the flesh can never bear this fruit, that you can never attain these things by your own effort, that they are "the fruit of the Spirit."'[2] It is the Holy Spirit who builds into our lives love, joy, peace, patience, kindness, goodness, faithfulness, gentleness and self-control (Gal. 5:22–23). Rather than asking us to try to be loving, patient and kind, God asks us to allow His Spirit to produce these qualities in our lives, enabling us to walk in the Spirit (Gal. 5:25), to journey in the Spirit. These are the journeying graces He calls us to pour into others.

As well as grace for the journey, the Spirit brings His gifts for guidance and spiritual direction. Along the way He comes with spiritual wisdom, knowledge, insight, understanding and enlightenment beyond our natural thinking, supernatural revelation and discernment. These are *parakletos* gifts, coming alongside gifts for the journey. Paul describes them as 'the supply of the Spirit' (Phil. 1:19). In one glorious flash of spiritual and supernatural intervention, the Holy Spirit can bring illumination, immense insight and understanding.

In relation to the past: 'But the Helper [*parakletos*] ... will ... bring to your remembrance all things that I have said to you' (John 14:26), all that He has already taught to us and revealed to us on our journey. It is through the testimony of God working in our lives that others understand the relevance of truth and grace to their lives.

In relation to the present: 'he will guide you into all truth' (John 16:13). As we seek to understand the stories of others He will impart wisdom, understanding and insight so they too come to know the truth, and that truth will set them free on their journey. In relation to the future: 'and he will tell you things to come' (John 16:13), meaning He will impart guidance and direction to help point us to the way forward, to the truth leading positively into the future.

## A guide into all truth

The Holy Spirit not only gives us graces, the fruit of the Spirit, but also truth: 'if I do not go away, the Helper [*parakletos*] will not come ... However, when He, the Spirit of truth, has come, He will guide you into all truth' (John 16:7,13). Notice that Jesus calls Him the Spirit of truth. He opens our understanding to the depth of God's revealed Word for our lives, bringing truth and guidance for the journey. We can learn about God's Word in Sunday school, church or even theological college. We can learn and read a great deal, but it is the illumination of the Holy Spirit Himself, the Spirit of truth who brings the revelation of living truth to God's Word. It is then that it becomes a light to our pathway and a lamp to our feet.

Jesus was now turning His teaching of the disciples over to the indwelling Spirit to lead them further into deeper understanding. '[T]he Helper [*parakletos*], the Holy Spirit, whom the Father will send in My name, He will teach you all things' (John 14:26). This 'all things' does not mean He imparts to us some kind of omniscience. 'All things' is used here in a relative sense, speaking of 'all things that *pertain* to life and godliness' (2 Pet. 1:3) needed for life's journey. For three years, Jesus had been teaching the disciples the Father's truth, but they never understood much. Now He would send a teacher who would dwell within them, taking the things of Jesus and revealing the truth of them. 'He will glorify Me, for he will take of what is Mine and declare *it* to you. All things that the Father has are Mine. Therefore I said that He will take care of Mine and declare *it* to You' (John 16:14–15).

## He will come 'upon you'

As we come alongside others, the Holy Spirit comes alongside us with His gifts, graces and truth to provide what we need to journey well. He takes our resource of journey from the natural (life experience) to the spiritual (received grace and truth) to the supernatural (revealed and applied by the Holy Spirit). The Holy Spirit takes and applies our resource of journey in a supernatural way, so that we're actually participating and partnering with Him in His work in the lives of others. It is the Holy Spirit who brings about change, not us.

After His resurrection Jesus again confirms the coming of the Holy Spirit using the third preposition 'come upon'. He then gives the clue as to the purpose of the Holy Spirit coming upon them: 'you shall receive power when the Holy Spirit has come upon you; and you shall be witnesses to me' (Acts 1:8). So the purpose of coming upon is that they would be empowered for the purpose of being 'witnesses to' Jesus. Not witnessing, but to be witnesses.

I don't know if you've been in a court of law, called to be a witness. You're asked to tell the truth, the whole truth, and nothing but the truth. What does a witness do? They truthfully and accurately recount details of their story, their recollection of the circumstance and facts of what happened. The advocate or the lawyer then takes their account and presents it for judgment. A witness simply tells the truth, recounting the facts of their journey as they understand them. That's what God calls us to in *paraclesis* – empowered by the Holy Spirit, we tell our story of Jesus through our resource of journey. Then the Holy Spirit, the advocate (*parakletos*), supernaturally reveals Jesus and applies grace and truth.

Jesus promised to send the disciples a divine advocate (*parakletos*) who would empower them to tell their Jesus story and share their journey powerfully with others. 'God's Way is not a matter of mere talk; it's an empowered life' (1 Cor. 4:20, MSG). As we join others on their journey, empowered to share our story, the Holy Spirit comes alongside with His gifts and His graces, leading, guiding and directing all into truth. Through His gifts and graces He reveals Jesus in our story. That's what telling our story and sharing our journey means – we are empowered to be living witnesses to Jesus.

## He will flow 'out of' you

Jesus said, 'He who believes in Me … as the Scripture has said, "From his innermost being will flow *continually* rivers of living water." But He was speaking of the [Holy] Spirit, whom those who believed in Him [as Saviour] were to receive' (John 7:38–39, AMP). The Holy Spirit's ministry through us is to enable us to pour out the water of life to others.

Our *paraclesis* verses in 2 Cor. 1:3–4 say: 'God of all comfort, who comforts us in all our tribulation, *that we may be able* to comfort those who are in any trouble' (my italics). The words 'that we may be able' or 'be enabled,' are from the Greek word *dynamai* the same root word Jesus used when He said the disciples would receive power (*dynamis*) after the Holy Spirit came upon them. It means the enabling power of the Holy Spirit flowing through us with encouragement, consolation, strength, comfort, spiritual direction, grace and truth. The Holy Spirit invites us to be partakers in ministry with Him, enabling us to be participators in His work. What a partnership to be in communion with the Holy Spirit. We are most like the Holy Spirit when we are coming alongside others, participating in *paraclesis*.

C.H. Spurgeon said, 'Without the Spirit of God, we can do nothing. We are as ships without the wind, branches without sap, and like coals without fire, we are useless'.[3] The apostle Paul said, 'I didn't try to impress you with polished speeches and the latest philosophy.

I deliberately kept it plain and simple … so nothing I said could have impressed you or anyone else. But the Message came through anyway. God's Spirit and God's power did it, which made it clear that your life of faith is a response to God's power, not to some fancy mental or emotional footwork by me or anyone else' (1 Cor. 2:1–5, MSG). The Holy Spirit will flow through you. So don't worry about what you're going to say. You'll find that as you listen to others' stories, the Holy Spirit's enabling will flow as you step out and recount your own story. Ignore any nervous feelings, draw on His enabling, and actively reach out, knowing the Holy Spirit will lead and guide you as only He can. In the NIV translation, Mark 13:11 says, 'do not worry beforehand about what to say. Just say whatever is given you at the time, for it is not you speaking, but the Holy Spirit'. This is the wonderful ministry and reality of the Holy Spirit coming alongside on the journey.

As we journey the Holy Spirit will be with us, in us, upon us, and will flow through us. I am told that a river which begins in the mountains of North Africa, never reaches its destination in the sea because it gets lost in the sands of the Sahara. If the Holy Spirit is not present on our journey we will get lost in the sands of surrounding circumstances. You can be sure that God is willing to do everything in His power to enable us to live the Spirit-filled life. He is willing to give as much of the Holy Spirit as we are willing to receive. So open your heart and life to a fresh flow of the Spirit as someone else needs that fresh flow of the Spirit, too.

CHAPTER 11

# Have you ever felt the need?

'"I was hungry and you gave Me food; I was thirsty and you gave Me drink; I was a stranger and you took Me in; I *was* naked and you clothed Me; I was sick and you visited Me; I was in prison and you came to Me." Then the righteous will answer Him, saying, "Lord, when did we see You hungry and feed *You*, or thirsty and give *You* drink ...?" And the King will answer ... "Assuredly, I say to you, inasmuch as you did *it* to one of the least of these My brethren, you did *it* to Me.' (Matt. 25:35–40)

There's a story about a police officer who pulled a driver over, and asks to see his driving licence. 'Is there something wrong, officer?' the driver asked. 'I didn't go through any red lights, and I certainly wasn't speeding.' 'No, you weren't', said the officer, 'but I saw you shaking your fist as you swerved around the lady driving in the left lane, and further observed your flushed, angry face as you shouted at the driver in the sports car who cut you off, and how you banged your steering wheel when the traffic came to a stop near the bridge.' 'Is that a crime, officer?'

'No', the officer replied, 'but when I saw the "Jesus loves you and so do I" sticker on the car, I figured this car must have be stolen.'[1] So much for car sticker evangelism!

Before we can effectively impact people by telling them God loves and cares for them, our deeds need to become as good as our doctrines. Demonstration must precede proclamation, authenticating the very message we bring. The fact of the matter is that we speak more by what we do than what we say (or put on car stickers). The old adage says, 'actions speak louder than words'. The gospel must first be evidenced by caring compassion. It's not that our message is not compelling but, as the driver of the car demonstrated, we are not always compelling messengers. One of the most effective ways to impact people today with the message of Jesus Christ is to meet them at the point of their need with honest, compassionate involvement.

## Connecting at the point of relevance

The final facet of our *paraclesis* diamond is the word 'entreat' or 'intreat': 'he was angry, and would not go in: therefore came his father out, and intreated [*parakaleo*] him' (Luke 15:28, KJV). It means to approach, reach out, connect, draw close, engage, persuade or plead. The prodigal son returned home to much rejoicing and great celebrations. His older brother, a faithful and loyal son, is angry about how his wayward brother is treated royally on his return. He goes outside, wanting nothing to do with it, so the father leaves the party and goes to 'intreat' him, to reach out to him, to invite him to come back in.

*Paraclesis* is reaching out, entreating those in our communities who are outside the family of God: the hurting, broken and needy in the neighbourhood around us. Our challenge is: will we connect with their needs or will we continue to preach to the choir? 'The Word became flesh and blood, and moved into the neighborhood' (John 1:14, MSG).

A felt need is the conscious need of the here and now. We can't meet every need we see, but people do want us to connect with them at the point of their felt need, the immediate need in front of them that they're currently struggling with. It is meeting them just where they are in the present moment. Jesus continually engaged and connected with people just where they were, in the moment.

Zacchaeus, lonely, friendless, hiding up a tree; the Samaritan woman at a well; five thousand hungry people on a hillside; a bereaved widow; grieving sisters; disconsolate disciples; a family in crisis at a wedding. Jesus engaged with felt needs not because He wanted people to follow Him, it was not a guise to inveigle them, but because He had compassion on them and wanted them to understand who He was – the Son of God. Most didn't follow Him but He still met their felt needs. He met them at the point of relevance.

The longer I pastor, the more I realize that in the fight for the kingdom of God, our arch nemesis isn't fighting liberalism, conservatism, secularism, pluralism, or any of the -isms at all – it's our irrelevance to people's felt needs. So many burning and acute issues of our day are pastoral care issues. People's lives and families are falling apart and they want to know and feel the relevance of the gospel to their need: 'Each one of us needs to look after the good of the people around us, asking ourselves, "How can I help?"' (Rom. 15:2, MSG).

## Felt needs lead to real needs

Connecting with felt needs leads to understanding real needs. The woman at the well came for water. What did Jesus talk about? Water. He connected at the point of felt need. It wasn't long before He was talking to her about her real thirst, the deep needs of her soul. Connecting at the point of felt need opens doors of opportunity. When most people are in need they aren't thinking about spiritual issues, but as we connect with felt needs they become sensitised to deeper spiritual needs that can only be fully met in the person of Jesus Christ.

I remember a businessman I met called Tony. Every so often I would go sailing with him. I got to know him and we journeyed together over several years. He had no faith and was a man of the world. He used to say to me, 'I don't understand you, Trevor, why you would want to sit round singing hymns, reading the Bible and praying. Get out, have some fun. Come with me and my pals to the races, back a few horses, have a few whiskies – we have great days out, you're missing out on life.' I would gently smile back and listen as he talked about his troubled marriage and family, his business problems and personal struggles. He was always talking about how great his pals were and all the wonderful times of golfing, sailing, drinking, womanising and gambling they enjoyed.

Then, early one morning I received a phone call – it was Tony, sobbing. He'd just discovered his wife dead in bed. I went immediately to the house and stood with him in the bedroom while we waited for the undertaker to arrive. I spent the following days with him and the family processing their bereavement, making funeral arrangements. His wife was a believer and with her loss, suddenly Tony's real needs came tumbling out. We shared and talked much together amidst his tears, pain and regrets. A few weeks later he came to Christ, was baptised, and some months later joined the local Baptist church. When the chips were down, somehow it wasn't these so-called wonderful pals he turned to in his hour of greatest need, but me. He told me some time later that my years of just being there for him, listening to his story and telling mine, were significant. His biggest regret was that his wife never saw him come to faith, and he was never able to share that part of his journey with her.

Each of us who have encountered Christ has a story to tell to those who don't know Him, of met needs, grace, mercy and triumph in adversity. You may say, 'But I was raised in church, I don't have a dramatic testimony.' It doesn't matter. Or, 'Nothing exciting has happened to me.' It doesn't matter. Your life's journey is the story of Jesus Christ working in all your life's circumstances since you met Him. That makes it important for someone who doesn't know Him. You may say, 'But I don't have much to offer', or, 'I'm nobody special'. Well, Jesus thought you are special enough to die for you, and to meet your deepest needs. You can't tell me that if the creator of the universe values you so much, your story and journey have no relevance. And it has eternal relevance for your neighbours and colleagues.

We can start to connect at the most basic levels of felt need. The kinds of need we come across in the daily course of our lives. Whether it's a neighbour who needs the grass mowed or a neighbour needing help with their groceries or children, or a colleague at work needing extra support. Entreating and reaching out don't mean inviting them to a special event or church meeting. It means connecting in the ordinary things of life, getting alongside. Your story – your life journey – is good news for someone.

## As my Father sent me, so I send you

Before ascending to His Father, Jesus came to His disciples, saying, 'As the Father has sent Me, I also send you' (John 20:21). For three years He'd journeyed together with them, connecting with people's lives. They'd been with Him, been part of His story, but now as He returns to His Father, He places this responsibility into their hands. He says to them, 'As you've been with me, now I am sending you to carry on in the same way' (my paraphrase). Someone described this as the Divine equation: 'as' He came alongside, cared and connected, 'so' He sends us to do the same. 'As' equals 'so'. Having ascended now to heaven, the mission of the gospel is committed to Jesus' followers. A new community culture, a new order is put in place. 'And all the believers lived in a wonderful harmony, holding everything in common. They sold whatever they owned and pooled their resources so that each person's need was met' (Acts 2:44–45, MSG).

Picking up the continuing story in Acts 3:1, 'Peter and John went up together to the temple at the hour of prayer', they come across a man at the gate Beautiful, the main entrance into the Temple. Many walk by this man daily as they enter 'church'. Even Peter and John had undoubtedly walked past him before. He's always at the gate, a paralysed beggar, 'lame from his mother's womb' (v2), severely disabled from birth. For years he had suffered from this chronic congenital disease, unable to stand or walk.

His disability is bad enough but something worse is going on. There were laws which forbade priests and Levites from serving God who were incapacitated or deformed in even little ways. Rabbinical laws and traditions prevented the crippled or paralysed from entering the Temple, God's House. His deformity meant he had to remain outside. The gate was the closest he got, so he was 'laid daily at the gate of the temple which is called Beautiful'. He's been there for many years, laying on the wrong side of the gate. No one could get him beyond it, not even religious people. He is marginalised by those who should care. There is no place for him in God's house.

It says that this man asked for 'alms from those who entered.' Almsgiving was an outward display of righteousness. He knew Temple people wanted to please God with a righteous act before going into His presence. If he begs for cash the likelihood is they'd give him some. I'm sure people wanted to feel righteous going to church, he simply manipulated and exploited their religion, they just fed his poverty. Because of what we know of the culture of the time, we can be quite certain that they gave him money only because it served their purposes, made them feel good about themselves. Sometimes we can do this in church. 'Lord, I won't go but here's the money to send someone else.' For the people on their way to the Temple who simply wanted to appear righteous, it was easier to throw a shekel to the man for their own purposes than to show any genuine care for his well-being.

## Engaging with felt needs

Verse 3 goes on to say that the man, 'seeing Peter and John about to go into the temple, asked for alms'. He had little choice but beg, depending on others. Beggars in those times normally had no education, nothing to put their hand to, they had little choice but to beg for money. A beggar represented one of lowest 'have nots' in society, generally thought to have no dignity, self-respect, or self-worth, they were despised and pitied. But Peter and John were in the new community, the new order.

They'd been with Jesus, seen Him connect at the point of felt need. Religion saw this crippled man as a problem but for them he was a man in need, kept outside the gates of the 'church'. These weren't average Temple-goers, they understood that felt needs lead to real needs.

His felt need was money, loose change, but they had none. It'd all gone into the common purse, put on the collection plate. That's what community means, giving everything for the common good of others. Now they had nothing except the power of Jesus' name. Other Temple-goers threw a shekel or two at the problem but Peter and John, belonging to a grace and truth community, recognised an opportunity: 'fixing his eyes on him, with John, Peter said, "Look at us"' (Acts 3:4). *The Message* says they, 'looked him straight in the eye', eye to eye contact, looking beyond a quick fix of a shekel or two.

Peter and John saw into the window of his soul to his deeper need, the pain, hurt, and rejection reflected in his eyes. They see him through eyes of compassion, eyes of love, eyes of grace, eyes of truth. This man was undoubtedly used to seeing eyes of disdain, contempt, pity, put-down, and humiliation as passers-by may have thrown their guilt money at him to appease their own conscience. But not these men. They 'entreated' him with eyes of warmth, understanding, and encouragement. Had they just responded to the problem like the others, they would simply have thrown a dinar or shekel. They see beyond the need for alms to his real need, the need to get him from outside to inside the gate, into God's presence.

Peter and John did not need to give alms in order to feel righteous, their righteousness was found in Christ. They weren't looking to receive righteousness through their actions, like the almsgivers, but to bring righteousness by their actions towards the man. They knew that money would only feed his poverty, keeping him in the same pattern outside the gate.

## Connecting with the real need

So they look him straight in the eye. Normally a beggar, when someone looks at them, looks beyond them to the next person, the next client, to to see where they can get more money. But it says he doesn't look beyond them, something about them arrested his attention and engaged him. He had been 'entreated' and 'he gave them his attention, expecting to receive something from them' (Acts 3:5). He looks at them with full attention. They convey hope, his expectation is 'something'. They had something he wanted and needed. Peter said, 'silver and gold I do not have, but what I do have I give you' (v6).

Thank God for social involvement, but let's be clear that the gospel is not a social gospel. Social is the point of connect, the felt need. If all we do is to relate to felt needs, we're no different to our secular counterparts or social agencies. The deep hunger and longing of the human soul is for spiritual reality. This is the real need. The experience of our journey tells us spiritual reality is found in Jesus. My business has gone bust, my kids went off the rails, my son's a drug addict, my family fell apart, but in the midst of it all the spiritual reality has been that the anchor for my soul is found in Jesus Christ. Peter and John knew the thing he longed for most was not money, but the ability to walk on healthy feet through that gate into God's presence that had been denied him for so long.

## Making available what we have

They look at this man knowing they haven't got what it takes to meet his felt need, but they're willing to make available what they do have to meet his real need, 'but such as I have give I thee' (v6, KJV). Obviously they didn't have money – it had all been given to the Church. They said, 'gold have I none; but *such* as I have give I thee' (my emphasis, v6, KJV). Wow, what a little word. We have nothing but '*such* as I have', in other words, what they *did* have they would give to him. Peter and John have their journey with Jesus, their presence, compassion, hope, and all that

Jesus had poured into them on their journey with Him to share with the beggar at the gate.

Remember, this is Peter the denier, who said, 'I do not know Him' (Luke 22:57). But something happened on his journey to transform him. He could now say with John, 'such as I have give I thee'. What is the 'such' you have? Your 'such' is your resource of journey, your life experience, the story of what God has been to you, what He's done for you. Bring it to God and say, 'This is my "such", it may not seem much, like the boy with the loaves and fishes; or the widow with the mite; or Mary with the alabaster jar. Not a lot, but it's Your "such"'. Let Him take it, and connect it with someone's felt need.

Don't look at what you don't have. They didn't let what they didn't have stop them reaching out with what they did have. Don't let the fear of what you don't have stop you connecting to others. Peter and John didn't have cash, but they had 'such'. Their lives weren't dictated by their limitations. Stop looking at your limitations – embrace your resource.

Realise what you do have. Recognise your 'such', your resource of journey, your experience of grace and truth. When you focus that, your own lack of ability, lack of confidence, experience, money or education, disappears. Your lack doesn't stop you passing on your journey to others. Embrace it with certainty. Peter and John had certainty about what they did have. When we have certainty about what we do have, we aren't limited by what we don't have, and when we make it available to God, He multiplies it. Your greatest liability can become your greatest asset in God's hand. Your mess becomes your message, your test your testimony. It's not your ability that counts but your availability, be willing to take the risk and trust God with the outcome.

## Empowered in Jesus' name

They boldly declare: 'In the name of Jesus Christ of Nazareth, rise up and walk', that name that's above every name, that name to which one day every knee will bow. I pray you come to the realisation that you're part of God's plan in this day and generation. God can take whatever's gone on in your life, no matter how low you've sunk, or how high you've risen, and use it in the name of Jesus Christ.

They gave him a hand up, not a hand out, 'he took him by the right hand and lifted *him* up, and immediately his feet and ankle bones received strength.' They reached out, took hold of his hand and lifted him to his feet. At that moment something flowed from them to him: supernatural strength, power, healing, deliverance from his condition, and the ability to enter the Temple. Instantly he felt it in his feet, ankles and legs. Never again would he be carried to the Temple gate. The name of Jesus always lifts people up and sets them on their journey again. 'So he, leaping up, stood and walked and entered the temple with them – walking, leaping and praising God' (v8). Leaping, dancing and rejoicing he enters into the courts of the Lord, singing praises to God and all the people were amazed.

They engaged in journey evangelism, taking the opportunity that day when everyone else walked by and threw their shekels. But it is as though they said, 'today we're going to *paraclesis* to entreat this man'. This is how the book of Acts began and we're the continuation of that story, that journey. Every day we have opportunities like Peter and John did to connect with the world of others, seeing life through their eyes. We can wake up with excitement and joy, because today we can reach out and help someone to stand up and get going on their journey again with new hope. This is the new order, empowered in Jesus' name to journey together with others. Reaching out from the House of God into our neighbourhood, taking *paraclesis* beyond the four walls of the church to those outside its gates, and impacting our communities.

## CHAPTER 12

# A 'coming alongside' community

'I want you to get out there and walk – better yet, run – on the road God called you to travel. I don't want any of you sitting around on your hands. I don't want anyone strolling off, down some path that goes nowhere. And mark that you do this with humility and discipline – not in fits and starts, but steadily, pouring yourselves out for each other in acts of love.' (Eph. 4:1–3, MSG)

Humpty Dumpty sat on a wall, Humpty Dumpty had a great fall; all the king's horses and all the king's men couldn't put Humpty together again. This chubby little guy walking down the street comes across a high wall. Although challenged by his size, height and shape he believes he can make it to the top. So with great effort, tenacity, endeavour and some difficulty he makes it to top of the pile. Sitting there, he surveys and muses on the world around him. We aren't informed as to what went wrong at this stage of his career, but whatever it was, it knocked him off and he crashes to the bottom of the pile, where his life is broken into a thousand pieces. He lays there at the bottom of the wall in utter disarray and confusion, a sad and sorry sight.

## A Humpty Dumpty world

If you think this story's about Humpty Dumpty, you'd be wrong, you've missed the point. It's about all the king's horses and the king's men. Humpty must've had friends of influence in high places. The king is quickly informed of his dreadful plight. He calls all his courtiers together to discuss the calamity. Immediately they decide it's of such gravity that all the king's horses (his entire stables) and all king's men (his entire staff) would be despatched immediately. Speedily, as fast as the horses would carry them, they arrive at the wall. Lights flashing, sirens blaring, horses neighing, dogs barking, but to no avail. The sad tragedy of the story is that despite all the finest resources the king could offer, they couldn't put Humpty together again. His brokenness was beyond all their best efforts. Not only was Humpty Dumpty humpty dumptied, but all the king's horses and all king's men were just as humpty dumptied as Humpty Dumpty. You don't need me to tell you that we live in a humpty dumpty world. Unfortunately, like all the king's men, even the best this world has to offer falls short at the foot of the wall.

Well, we don't have the king's horses but we are all the King's men (and women), summoned by the King to the foot of the wall. From the foot of the wall we can journey with the broken and bruised to the foot of the cross. Why? Because we've journeyed that way before ourselves. We're part of a new kingdom that specialises in the Humpty Dumpties of this world, an alternative community, a culture of care. We have the resources in Christ among us to mend broken hearts, restore broken lives and heal broken bodies. There are countless living witnesses to this in our churches. Lives have been mended, healed, restored and made strong again at the broken places. We all have Humpy Dumpty stories to tell, and can thank God they didn't end up broken at the foot of a wall, but ended up restored at the foot of a cross.

## Back to our roots

You're getting the picture here. Now more than ever the Church needs to be a *paracletic* community at the bottom of the wall. Not a club for the blessed but a hospital for the broken. We need to come back to our roots on this one. The Church has historically provided pastoral care in the community, and been the first at the foot of the wall.

It was the Church that reached out to the Humpty Dumpties of this world. The Samaritans started in church; Relate (marriage guidance) started in church; Alcoholics Anonymous started with the church; the hospice movement started with the church; Chaplaincy services, YMCA and Toc H, all began with the church, (I could go on and on here). All these organisations began with people who had a resource of journey and were willing to engage with others. Around AD 360 Emperor Julian claimed: 'the impious Galileans [Christians] support not only their own poor but ours as well, all men see that our people lack aid from us.'[1] It was said that some civil institutions closed because Christians had taken the poor and sick into their own homes. This was a jewel in the Church's crown. Chuck Colson said, 'I think the local church has to be responsible for making the invisible kingdom visible.'[2]

Could it be with the rise and development of professional services, mental health care and the burgeoning behavioural sciences and counselling movements in recent years, that the Church has relinquished its role of providing genuine community pastoral care? I think sometimes we get sidetracked by the voices of modern-day psychology, of Freud, Janov, Skinner, Rogers, Jung, among many other gurus of the behavioural sciences. Maybe we need to pay more attention to the words of wisdom of Jesus, Paul, Peter, James and John. With all the focus on personal mentors, life coaches, professional counsellors, psychotherapists, mental health experts, social workers, spiritual directors and the modern breed of pastorpreneurs, I often wonder whether or not Church pastoral care is now being pushed to the margins of irrelevancy.

## The priesthood of all believers

Could it be we've lost sight of our God-given calling, the basic New Testament 'one another' approach to pastoral care that Jesus first taught His disciples, that became so seminal and central in early Church life. We all have the priestly role to play of coming before God on behalf of men, and coming before men on behalf of God. God has made every believer a priest and minister, He 'has made us kings and priests' (Rev. 1:6). We are all in the priesthood of believers. Jesus is our High Priest: 'we have a Priest-Friend [*parakletos*] in the presence of the Father: Jesus Christ' (1 John 2:1, MSG).

Maybe we need to revisit again a basic understanding of our ecclesiology as it relates to 'one another', *paraclesis*, and the priesthood of all believers: 'you also, as living stones, are being built up *as* a spiritual house, a holy priesthood' (1 Pet. 2:5).

The priesthood of all believers has dogged the Church's footsteps for centuries. So much so, it was one of the three tenets that formed the Reformation (under Martin Luther) that Protestantism was founded on. It's what the 'protest' was about, and in my view the priesthood of all believers has been the most neglected central teaching of the Reformation. Martin Luther believed, 'this word priest should become as common as the word Christian'.[3] Luther maintained that the ploughboy and milkmaid could do priestly work; in fact, their ploughing and milking *was* priestly work, tasks that were part of their journey.

This notion that all believers are ministering priests would revolutionise how we carry out pastoral care, we'd truly become the 'coming alongside' *paracletic* community. Alastair Campbell, a Scottish professor and theologian, uses the term, 'the pastorhood of all believers' and says, 'Pastoral care … is not correctly understood if it is viewed within the framework of professionalism … Pastoral care is a relationship founded upon the integrity of the individual. Such a relationship does not depend primarily upon the acquisition of knowledge or the development of skill. Rather it depends on a caring attitude towards others which comes from our own experience of pain, fears, and loss and our own release from their deadening grip'.[4]

## The challenge of pastoral care

If you take the view, as I do, that *paraclesis* is pastoral care; that 'one another' pastoral care is everyone's responsibility; that 'the priesthood of all believers' includes all laypeople; that pastoral care is not the sole domain of the professionals, then together we can face the challenge of being a community of care. Together we can nurture the culture of *paraclesis* 'coming alongside' pastoral care, with people in the pews being 'one another' ministers.

The New Testament speaks of 'one another' care and concern over sixty times. We're called to be a 'coming alongside', journeying together community. Side by side we can change the front door, back door syndrome, address layer-to-layer fellowship, and eliminate snooker table church. With the wealth of the untapped resource of life experience among us, together we can minister and reach out to our neighbourhoods at the point of felt need. We can see ourselves again as being significant and primary contributors to the mainstream of local life. Together, we can step out of the shadows and reclaim our traditional and vital pastoral care role in today's society.

If I read the New Testament correctly it appears God's main agency in society is the Church, His plan A, the only organism able to represent God's character at work. I'm not sure I can find a plan B. We're all part of one another, it's what the body of Christ is about. God calls us to journey together in life. So how can we work this out in reality? What is the relationship between clergy, laity and professionals? Here's my overview. I see pastoral care at three levels: primary, secondary and tertiary.

## Primary care

The main focus of our attention is to be healthy, whole, and full of vitality and energy. Every good parent gives attention to growing strong, healthy, mature, well-rounded children. Ensuring a wholesome, nutritious, balanced diet, contributing to welfare and wellbeing in a safe and secure environment. Creating an enriching culture, enabling them to reach their full potential, maximise their personal development, realise fully their individual abilities and achieve their dreams. Encouraging, affirming and valuing them; equipping, teaching and guiding them for life; enabling them to make their way in the world with impact and personal fulfilment.

It's not dissimilar in the Church. The shepherd/leader's pastoral role sets the culture of spirituality, nurturing and growing the flock/congregation to spiritual health and maturity, supporting them through all the stages of life. Caring for people's spiritual welfare. Feeding, teaching, preaching, leading them individually and as a congregation so their lives have impact and fulfilment in God's purposes. Seeing them reach their full potential in Christ. Setting into the culture and environment all of the infrastructures necessary to enable people to care for one another, 'so that God's people would be *thoroughly* equipped to minister and build up the body of the Anointed One' (Eph. 4:12, TV). In most churches the primary care responsibility is more than a full-time role.

## Secondary care

Even healthy people face health challenges; maybe a common cold, a bout of the flu, a sudden virus, a thumping headache, or an unforeseen accident around the home. At some point illness and sickness of one sort or another strikes. At these times we need someone with knowledge and understanding to point us to a solution, to journey with us in the moment, someone who's processed the challenge and found a remedy. These aren't life-threatening challenges but common health issues we all contend with. Sometimes it means a visit to the medicine cabinet, the first aid kit, the wisdom of a mother, the advice of a friend, or a visit to the doctor or pharmacy.

So it is in life, all is going swimmingly when sudden unexpected circumstances overtake and overwhelm us: redundancy, bereavement, disappointment, marriage and family struggles or financial setbacks. Those times when we need someone with some experience, understanding and insight to journey with us. We're not in need of professional counselling, a mentor, life coach or psychotherapist, we're needing someone with a resource of journey that relates to us. The shepherd/pastor/leader who is already stretched to the limits needs to be able to point members of the flock in the direction of those who can come alongside, understand and care, functioning under the umbrella of the church's spiritual oversight. This is the secondary level of care. Pastor Gareth Crossley says, 'A golden rule for pastors is, never do the work of general ministry that can be done by others. Pastoral leadership consists principally in learning how to empower, enable and enrich... others.'[5]

## Tertiary care

There come times when chronic illness and disease overtake our lives: a heart attack, cancer, kidney failure, glaucoma, diabetes, a car accident, needing specialist medical attention, expert treatment, possibly surgery or intensive care. They're beyond the realm of common health challenges and need someone with appropriate training, specific skills, expertise and qualification in their field.

So it is on the journey of life, things happen that are beyond the common life issues and are seriously debilitating. Deep traumas, personality disorders, eating disorders, obsessive-compulsive behaviours, physical, sexual and psychological abuse, addictions of all kinds, deep depression. These need more expert understanding and is where professional counselling comes into its own. These deeper issues of personality require on-going counselling that takes time, and professional support often needing long-term recovery. This is normally beyond the understanding and expertise of the shepherd/pastor/leader and the level of secondary care. This is tertiary care.

## Soul care

Could it be that if we journeyed effectively with people at the level of secondary care, 'coming alongside', many would not be in need of a professional counsellor? It seems that as soon as someone is struggling with an issue of life today, they're told they need to see a counsellor. Unfortunately, referring people to the professionals is becoming the standard default position. Somehow many have come to equate pastoral care as being the same as professional counselling. Renowned Christian psychologist Dr Larry Crabb makes a perceptive observation, 'For a surgeon to abandon his practice in order to study nutrition would at first glance seem to be an unreasonable thing to do. The shift would make little sense unless the doctor had good reason to suspect that good eating habits could actually reverse disease more powerfully and quickly than surgery. Then by studying nutrition the surgeon would be working toward the day when invasive, hard to schedule operations would no longer be necessary, when vegetables not scalpels would do the job.' [6] Much of our pastoral care has become reactive, that's to say, we allow the situation to deteriorate before sending for the professionals. To use Larry Crabb's analogy, we send for the surgeon because we failed to put in place the nutritionist.

Let's be clear, counselling is not pastoral care. Although it may be part of it at the tertiary level, it's not a replacement for primary and secondary care. Dr Larry Crabb also says, 'There is no meaningful distinction between psychological and spiritual problems, only between physical and personal problems. Personal problems require personal care or pastoral care. I suggest that soul care can best be provided within spiritual community.' [7] The Church, the Body of Christ, is that spiritual community, that 'coming alongside' community, not a counselling agency. We're called to be ministers of grace and truth, not spiritual therapists. Pastoral care is coming alongside people in the context of community life together, a caring *paracletic* community based around fellowship, and ministering to one another; not a healing ministry but a healing community. There's no question in my mind that if there were more effective secondary pastoral care networks functioning in our congregations, there would be less focus on professional counselling.

I've often asked myself how the Church has ever survived throughout the ages without of all these modern specialists. Does the responsibility really lie with the professionals and specialists, or have we relinquished some of our God-given commission and purpose as the Body of Christ into their hands?

I've also wondered sometimes whether we've been bamboozled by the explosion of the behavioural sciences and secular and Christian counselling movements. In recent years they have become a significant growth industry. Is it possible we've bought into the philosophy that what we need in the Church is not better pastoral care and community systems, but more professional counsellors on staff? Has this growth industry assumed such an exaggerated sense of importance, that secondary pastoral care in the context of Christian community has been largely consigned to the annals of Church history? Could it be that now is the time to redress the balance between pastoral care and professional counselling?

Bruce Larson says, 'Healing is not the province of the specialized few; a secular study some years ago proved that. It was done to determine which school of counselling—Rogerian, Freudian, Jungian, and so on—produced the best results. The results were intriguing. The most effective counselling was provided not by the disciples of any of these professional schools, but by the control groups used in the study. Ordinary people—airline pilots, secretaries, housewives, businesspersons—with no therapy training, who simply spent time listening, produced better results than the professionals. It has been said that only about one person in ten seeking counselling has special needs requiring professional help. The other 90 per cent are well served by talking to a sympathetic layperson.'[8]

## A journeying community

After five years pastoring in New Zealand, Deb and I returned to the UK. A few months later, I received a call from the Rev Dr Craig Heilmann. 'Trev', he said, 'God's called Kim and I to pioneer a new work in Auckland. We've two families joining, supporting and standing with us. We want you to come and join with us on the pastoral care side.' Craig and I had previously journeyed together and our hearts were in tune. Deb and I returned to Auckland to join Craig, Kim, their three boys, and the other two families. The small group started meeting in an upper room on the edge of Newmarket on the outskirts of the city. Our journey together would continue, me giving focus on pastoral care alongside Craig's leadership, planting and growing the church. Over the weeks and months others came and we started meeting in a local school hall.

Our goal was to be a community church, a journeying church with a culture of 'one another' caring and a *paraclesis* ethos reaching into the community. It was a work in progress as we started to journey with people. Jason and Tatiana joined us early on, battered and bruised by those who should have cared. They were disillusioned and dispirited. I recall them saying they'd decided not to attend another church again. We journeyed with them, and over the five years the church has been going we've seen them grow and develop, now making a significant impact in the community.

We hadn't been long in the school hall when Alasdair came one Sunday morning. Alasdair had just resigned from being head of the Employers and Manufacturers Association (equivalent to head of the Confederation of British Industry). A media firestorm had broken out around him, forcing him out. He was being interviewed on TV and made what some considered an unwise controversial gender statement about women in the workplace. It became a massive news story. The fallout was enormous. His world fell apart as he was hounded in the press by all. He was devastated and publicly humiliated. His was a Humpty Dumpty story of the biggest proportions. A local GP,

Dr Hilmar Budelmann, who had started attending with us, found him at the bottom of the wall and pointed him in our direction. An ebullient character with strong views, he would heckle and question the speakers at the front on a Sunday morning. After some months with us, he came to faith, and we journeyed with him. He has now written a book of his experience and transformation called *Life Changing* and is reaching out to businessmen who face similar challenges.

Raewyn and Denis also joined us in the school. The day they came Raewyn said, 'There's something here that makes us feel this is our spiritual home.' We journeyed with them through Raewyn's deep struggle with anxiety, and her subsequent freedom from it. Today Raewyn leads a community group for young mums called Sojourners and an outreach to women facing issues post-abortion, called You Are Not Alone, and Denis leads ICONZ, a support and outreach programme for 8–10-year-old boys.

Alex turned up at the school hall one Sunday morning early on. His life was a mess. He was in a dark and difficult place. With two failed marriages, he was also struggling with alcohol and other issues, including a dysfunctional family background; truly another Humpty Dumpty story. Over many months, despite setbacks, we journeyed with Alex until he made a breakthrough and started to get his life back on track. Finding spiritual direction, he went back to college, studied hard, is soon to graduate and has some informal roles with Maori and Polynesian groups in Auckland.

After 18 months we outgrew the school, with standing room only. We found an old warehouse with a demolition order on it. It's all we could afford. A new part of the journey started as we acquired a lease and set about transforming it into our new home. Over six months, work parties toiled and grafted, spending weekends and evenings ripping it apart and putting it together again. Generous gifts were given to make it possible. 'One another' connections and journeys were formed, the culture of our community was being set.

It's still a work in progress, but now five years on, The Upper Room Church, Newmarket, Auckland, is a community of over 600. To develop the journeying culture, I devised a teaching and equipping church series, involving Sunday sermons, a *Daily Guide* workbook, and small group materials for the entire church to be involved. I called it Paraclesis: Journeying Together. Churches around the world can now take part in this six-week (42-day) series, helping their congregations come alongside others. More information on how to find out more can be found in the back of this book.

After Alasdair wrote his book, such was the change in him that national TV made a programme about him. As part of his journey, they filmed him alongside his wife Joan worshipping God in our old warehouse church. Part of our community journey was now being broadcast around the country. There are so many more stories of 'coming alongside' to tell – others like these – if only I had space, but that would take another book.

# Epilogue

As you will have read, *Love With Skin On* is my attempt to introduce you to what I believe is a missing jewel in the Church, *paraclesis* – 'coming alongside others'. The heart behind this book is not to just provide you with information, but to motivate and mobilise you to actively be 'love with skin on'.

You now have the opportunity to respond and identify the unique experiences with Christ that you have encountered on your life's journey. Then, like Jesus on the road to Emmaus, you will be able to effectively come alongside others to console, comfort, entreat, exhort and encourage them on their own journeys. You may wish to learn more about the accompanying six-week church series, Paraclesis: Journeying Together, which is explained further at the back of this book.

If you're one of those who are currently struggling along the way, seek out those who will be able to come alongside and journey with you. With God's healing comfort, and their support, you can be strengthened in your time of need and become someone who comes alongside others.

> 'All praise to the God and Father of our Master, Jesus the
> Messiah! Father of all mercy! God of all healing counsel!
> He comes alongside us when we go through hard times, and
> before you know it, he brings us alongside someone else who
> is going through hard times so that we can be there for that
> person just as God was there for us. We have plenty of hard
> times that come from following the Messiah, but no more
> so than the good times of his healing comfort – we get a full
> measure of that, too.' (2 Cor. 1:3–4, MSG)

# Endnotes

**Introduction**
[1] From the hymn 'Christ is the Answer to my Every Need' by William T. Maltby (Copyright 1945 Salvationist Publishing and Supplies Ltd).

**Chapter 1**
[1] J. MacArthur, *Philippians* (Chicago: Moody Press, 2001).

[2] Headline taken from article by Katy Winter (9 January 2014), *Mail Online* [http://www.dailymail.co.uk/femail/article-2536597/Were-selfie-obsessed-Over-17-million-self-portraits-uploaded-social-media-week-55s-taking-aged-18-24.html] (accessed March 2016).

[3] Cited in Sam Majdi, *The Wisdom of the Great* (Bloomington, IN, USA: iUniverse, 2012), p227.

[4] John D. Zizioulas, *Communion and Otherness: Further Studies in Personhood and the Church* (London: T&T Clark, 2009).

[5] Stephen R. Covey, *The 7 Habits of Highly Effective People: Powerful Lessons in Personal Change* (New York: Free Press, 2004), pp30—31.

[6] Cited by Katherine Pilnick, '13 Powerful and Inspirational Quotes by Will Smith', *Wall Street Insanity*, 20 January 2014. Found at [http://wallstreetinsanity.com/13-powerful-and-inspirational-quotes-from-will-smith/] (accessed March 2016).

**Chapter 2**
[1] *My Big Fat Greek Wedding*. Dir. Joel Zwick. USA: Gold Circle Films, 2002.

[2] Charles Spurgeon, 'Consolation in Christ: A Sermon', *The Complete Works of C. H. Spurgeon, Volume 7: Sermons 348—426* (USA: Delmarva Publications, 2013).

[3] Cited in Dave and Tina Samples, *Messed Up Men of the Bible: Seeing the Men in Your Life Through God's Eyes* (Grand Rapids, MI, USA: Kregel Publications), p130.

[4] Cited by David Young, *Breakthrough Power: A Daily Guide to an Extraordinary Life* (Round Rock, TX, USA: Wind Runner Press, 2009), p120.

[5] From *Holwick's Illustrations* [http://www.holwick.com/], cited on *WITandWisdom* by Richard Wimer [www.witandwisdom.org]. Author's source: [http://www.actsweb.org/articles/article.php?i=1398&d=2&c=3] (accessed March 2016).

[6] Song lyrics from 'Ah Lord God' by Don Moen, from the album *Give Thanks* (Integrity Music: 1986).

[7] Quotation attributed to John Watson (also known by the name of Ian Maclaren), AD 1850—1907 (public domain).

**Chapter 3**
[1] Taken from the character Charlie Brown from the comic strip series 'Peanuts' (USA: 1950—2000), created by Charles M. Shultz (AD 1922—2000).

[2] Orison Swett Marden, *Peace Power & Plenty* (New York: Cosimo, Inc., 2007), p29.

[3] John Powell, *Why Am I Afraid to Tell You who I Am?: Insights into Personal Growth* (Zondervan, 1999), p12.

[4] Taken from the classic Western (USA) song 'Home on the Range'. Original lyrics believed to be by Brewster M. Higley, circa 1870.

[5] Rick Warren, 'Some Cures for Discouragement', CBN (2016). Found at [www1.cbn.com/biblestudy/some-cures-for-discouragement] (accessed March 2016).

[6] Cited in R. T. Kendall, *Why Jesus Died: A meditation on Isaiah 53* (Oxford: Monarch Books, 2011), p52.

**Chapter 4**
[1] Cited in Selwyn Hughes, *The Seven Laws of Spiritual Success* (Nashville, TN, USA: Broadman & Holman Publishers, 2005), p126.

[2] Cited in Terry R. Lynch, *Prayer: Teach us to Pray* (Terry R. Lynch: 2013).

[3] Bruce Larson, Paul Anderson and Doug Self, *Mastering Pastoral Care* (Multnomah Press, 1990), p128.

[4] Ignatius Fernandez, *Through the Eye of a Needle: Transforming Relationships* (New Delhi: Sterling Publishers, 2007), p144.

**Chapter 5**
[1] *Forrest Gump.* Dir. Robert Zemeckis. USA: Paramount, 1994.

[2] Alex Elle, also known as Alexandra L. Smith [www.alexelle.info]. Found at [https://www.goodreads.com/quotes/1177779] (accessed March 2016).

[3] Famous African proverb. Cited in Richard Stearns, *Unfinished: Filling the Hole in Our Gospel* (Nashville, TN, USA: Thomas Nelson, 2013), p136.

[4] Vera Nazarian, *The Perpetual Calendar of Insipiration* (Norilana Booksm 2010).

[5] Taken from a sermon by Ray C. Steadman, 'Why does it Hurt so Much?' (Peninsula Bible Church, 16 September 1979). Found at [https://www.pbc.org/system/message_files/4941/3676.html] (accessed March 2016).

[6] Cited in Les Parrott and Leslie Parrott, *The One Year Love Talk Devotional for Couples* (in association with Yates & Yates, 2011).

[7] Cited in Joyce Meyer, *Change Your Words, Change Your Life: Understanding the Power of Every Word You Speak* (London: Hodder and Stoughton, 2012).

**Chapter 6**
[1] Ursula K. Le Guin, *The Left Hand of Darkness* (Great Britain: Gollancz, 1969).

[2] Oxford English Dictionary ('narrative'). Public domain.

[3] From the poem 'To a Mouse' by Robert Burns, 1785.

**Chapter 7**
[1] Lyrics from the hymn 'In the Garden', by C. Austin Miles (circa 1912).

**Chapter 8**
[1] C. S. Lewis, *The Pilgrim's Regress* (copyright C. S. Lewis Pte Ltd, 1933). Used with permission.

[2] Mathew Henry's Commentary on John 5, *Bible Hub* (2016), found at [http://biblehub.com/commentaries/mhc/john/5.htm] (accessed March 2016).

[3] William Glasser, M.D., *Reality Therapy: A New Approach to Psychiatry* (New York: Harper & Row, 1965).

[4] Jimmy Dean, found at [http://www.brainyquote.com/quotes/quotes/j/jimmydean131287.html] (accessed March 2016).

[5] Viktor E. Frankl, *Man's Search for Meaning: An Introduction to Logotherapy* (London: Hodder and Stoughton Ltd, 1964).

[6] Lao Tzu, circa 5th century BC, Zhou Dynasty (public domain).

[7] Stephen R. Covey, *The 7 Habits of Highly Effective People: Powerful Lessons in Personal Change* (New York: Free Press, 2004).

## Chapter 9
[1] Ernest Hemingway, *A Farwell to Arms* (USA: Scribner, 1929).

[2] According to Roy D. Altman, MD, 'Anklyosing Spondylitis', *MSD Manual Online*, 2016. Found at [http://www.msdmanuals.com/en-gb/professional/musculoskeletal-and-connective-tissue-disorders/joint-disorders/anklyosing-spondylitis] (accessed March 2016).

[3] Song lyrics taken from 'He Touched Me', by Vincent Youmans, Billy Rose and Edward Eliscu (Warner/Chappell Music, Inc., 1964). Found at [http://www.songfacts.com/detail.php?lyrics=15362] (accessed March 2016).

## Chapter 10
[1] D.L. Moody, AD 1837—1899 (public domain). Found at [http://www.goodreads.com/quotes/198756-the-best-way-to-show-that-a-stick-is-crooked] (accessed March 2016).

[2] R.A. Torrey, 'The Holy Spirit Bringing Forth in the Believer Christlike Graces of Character', *Bible Hub*, 2016. Found at [http://biblehub.com/library/torrey/the_person_and_work_of_the_holy_spirit/chapter_xiii_the_holy_spirit.htm] (accessed March 2016).

[3] From Charles H. Spurgeon's sermon 'A Revival Promise', delivered 11 January 1874 at The Metropolitan Tabernacle, Newington.

## Chapter 11
[1] Story taken from *Preaching Today*, 2016, found at [http://www.preachingtoday.com/illustrations/2005/june/16009.html] (accessed March 2016).

## Chapter 12
[1] Finley Hooper and Matthew Schwartz, *Roman Letters: History from a Personal Point of View* (Detroit, MI, USA: Wayne State University Press, 1991), p142.

[2] Charles Colson and Gabe Lyons, 'Chuck Colson's Legacy in His Own Words', *Q Ideas*, 2014. Article found at http://qideas.org/articles/chuck-colsons-legacy-in-his-own-words/ (accessed March 2016).

[3] Martin Luther, *The Epistles of St. Peter and St. Jude: Preached and Explained* (New York: Anson D.F. Randolph, 1859).

[4] Alastair V. Campbell, *Rediscovering Pastoral Care* (Darton, Longman & Todd, 1986), p41.

[5] Gareth Crossley, 'Counselling: Pastoral Care or Psychotherapy?', found at [www.affinity.org.uk] (accessed March 2016).

[6] Larry Crabb, *Connecting: Healing Ourselves and Our Relationships* (Nashville, TN, USA: W Publishing Group, 1990), p12.

[7] Larry Crabb, *The Safest Place on Earth: Where People Connect and Are Forever Changed* (Nashville, TN, USAA: W Publishing Group, 1990), p9.

[8] Bruce Larson, Paul Anderson and Doug Self, *Mastering Pastoral Care* (Multnomah Press, 1990), p130.

Having read the message behind *paraclesis* and the gift of journey each of us has to offer – you may like to consider introducing Paraclesis: Journeying Together to your church.

**paraclesis**
*Coming alongside others*

# How to start your journey

1.  **WHO CARES?**
    **Visit** the Paraclesis website to discover more about Paraclesis: Journeying Together and how your church can sign up to come alongside others.

2.  **DO YOU CARE?**
    **Sign-up** to explore how you and your church can care. You will receive a free Introduction Pack, including an Introductory Booklet and a DVD with videos perfect for introducing Paraclesis: Journeying Together to your church leadership team. Once your leadership team have explored whether Paraclesis: Journeying Together is suitable for your church the next step is to register.

3.  **MY CHURCH CARES!**
    **Register** your church to fully participate in the Paraclesis initiative and become a Paraclesis Church! For just £25 you will receive a Sample Pack, including another full copy of *Love with Skin On* and of the companion workbook the *Daily Guide*, flyers, postcards, a wristband and a kindness box. You will also gain full access to all of the online resources accompanying the six-week series.

You and your church will now be ready to journey together ...

Courses and seminars

Waverley Abbey College

Publishing and media

Conference facilities

# Transforming lives

CWR's vision is to enable people to experience personal transformation through applying God's Word to their lives and relationships.

Our Bible-based training and resources help people around the world to:
• Grow in their walk with God
• Understand and apply Scripture to their lives
• Resource themselves and their church
• Develop pastoral care and counselling skills
• Train for leadership
• Strengthen relationships, marriage and family life and much more.

Our insightful writers provide daily Bible-reading notes and other resources for all ages, and our experienced course designers and presenters have gained an international reputation for excellence and effectiveness.

CWR's Training and Conference Centres in Surrey and East Sussex, England, provide excellent facilities in idyllic settings – ideal for both learning and spiritual refreshment.

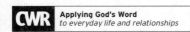
**CWR** Applying God's Word
to everyday life and relationships

CWR, Waverley Abbey House,
Waverley Lane, Farnham,
Surrey GU9 8EP, UK

Telephone: **+44 (0)1252 784700**
Email: **info@cwr.org.uk**
Website: **www.cwr.org.uk**

Registered Charity No. 294387
Company Registration No. 1990308